LEAD

FROM THE

FUTURE

LEAD
FROM THE
FUTURE

*How to Turn Visionary Thinking
into Breakthrough Growth*

MARK W. JOHNSON
JOSH SUSKEWICZ

HARVARD BUSINESS REVIEW PRESS
BOSTON, MA

Copyright 2020 Mark W. Johnson and Josh Suskewicz
All rights reserved
Printed in the United States of America

10 9 8 7 6 5 4 3 2 1

No part of this publication may be reproduced, stored in or introduced into a retrieval system, or transmitted, in any form, or by any means (electronic, mechanical, photocopying, recording, or otherwise), without the prior permission of the publisher. Requests for permission should be directed to permissions@harvardbusiness.org, or mailed to Permissions, Harvard Business School Publishing, 60 Harvard Way, Boston, Massachusetts 02163.

The web addresses referenced in this book were live and correct at the time of the book's publication but may be subject to change.

Library of Congress Cataloging-in-Publication Data

Names: Johnson, Mark W., author. | Suskewicz, Josh, author.
Title: Lead from the future : how to turn visionary thinking into breakthrough
    growth / Mark W. Johnson and Josh Suskewicz.
Description: Boston, MA : Harvard Business Review Press, [2020] | Includes index. |
Identifiers: LCCN 2019046716 (print) | LCCN 2019046717 (ebook) |
    ISBN 9781633697546 (hardcover) | ISBN 9781633697553 (ebook)
Subjects: LCSH: Transformational leadership. | Forecasting. | Creative ability
    in business. | Success in business.
Classification: LCC HD57.7 .J64375 2020 (print) | LCC HD57.7 (ebook) |
    DDC 658.4/092–dc23
LC record available at https://lccn.loc.gov/2019046716
LC ebook record available at https://lccn.loc.gov/2019046717

The paper used in this publication meets the requirements of the American National Standard for Permanence of Paper for Publications and Documents in Libraries and Archives Z39.48-1992.

Contents

A Tribute to a True Visionary
Clayton M. Christensen (1952-2020)

As a teacher, collaborator, partner, colleague, role model, and, most important, friend for twenty-five years, Clayton Christensen did more to shape my way of thinking than anyone else. This book would never have come to be without our close and profound association.

For me, Clay embodied what it means to lead from the future. His seminal theory of disruption stems from a fundamental understanding: that when business leaders develop and utilize good theory, their efforts in strategy and innovation (and, indeed, in managing the dynamics of their whole industries) can become much more predictable. I think of the theory that undergirds *Lead from the Future* in much the same way. Leaders can use it to put themselves in an envisioned future, frame its circumstances as a "situation I'm in," and then develop clear-eyed views about the most effective ways to innovate within it.

Clay also taught me that the strength of his theories is not simply that they make businesses more predictable, and hence profitable. The nonconsumers that disruptors serve and benefit are often the less fortunate in society. At root, business disruption enables, as Clay put it, "a larger population of less-wealthy or less-skilled people to do things for themselves in more convenient, less centralized, less expensive settings." Clay was onto something way ahead of his time—that good business is not just about making more profits for shareholders but serving stakeholders of every kind—that the best-run companies, in the words of the Business Roundtable's recent statement on the purpose of a corporation, deliver value to customers, invest in their employees, and support the communities in which they work.[1]

But disruption theory is even more profound than that. Ultimately, it is not just about democratizing products and services but empowering people to grow and flourish. Clay's book *How Will You Measure Your Life?* provides the most fascinating application of its transcendent power as it moves from helping companies to helping individuals achieve better outcomes in their lives and relationships, one by one.

Our present and future are as challenging and indeed as frightening as they've ever been; we have a desperate need for visionaries. Clay Christensen was such a one—a prophet ahead of his time, who mastered the doctrine of management from the future.

I honor his life's work and dedicate this book to him.

Mark W. Johnson
Belmont, Massachusetts
January 2020

LEAD FROM THE FUTURE

Where there is no vision, the people perish.

—Proverbs 29:18

Everyone recognizes a great, visionary leader when they see one—at least in retrospect, after their prescient ideas have been borne out by time. In history, Winston Churchill inspired the British in their darkest hour, and Nelson Mandela led the resistance to apartheid from his prison cell on Robben Island. Visionary industrial-age titans like Thomas Edison, Henry Ford, and Kiichiro Toyoda, and, in our own day, Bill Gates, Steve Jobs, and Jeff Bezos recognized the transformative power of new technologies and leveraged them to build vast enterprises that changed whole economies and ways of life. Each of these leaders looked past the conventional wisdom of their day, foresaw a different and better world, and mobilized others to join them in their quests to create it.

Where did their vision come from? By what alchemy, besides sheer force of intellect, personality, and determination, did they bring them to life? Visionary business leaders, we are told, are usually entrepreneurs who build their organizations from scratch; rarely, if ever, are they found at established organizations. Most, we have been led to believe, are creatures we can only admire and never hope to emulate, who are gifted with a mysterious power of second sight that lets them see opportunities where others cannot.

That is not what we think. As business strategists who specialize in helping firms navigate disruptive change and develop future-oriented growth strategies, we have learned that visionaries are simply flesh-and-blood human beings who have figured out how to develop actionable views of their organizations' best possible futures—views that are clear-eyed, inspiring, and granular enough that they can be operationalized, which is to say, directly linked to an explicit strategic path that starts in the here and now. We believe that the ability to develop and then actualize such a vision is a critical—perhaps *the* critical—executive skill, though it is sorely neglected in traditional management doctrine.

When he was a young man, Apple's Steve Jobs experimented with LSD and lived in an ashram in India. We're not going to tell you that we have a formula that will allow you to do all the things that he did—at the beginning, in that fabled garage in Los Altos, and years later, when he transformed Apple into the giant enterprise that it is today. But we can tell you that you don't have to take mind-altering drugs to become more visionary.

Developing and deploying an inspiring and actionable vision is a skill that can be learned. Beyond that, it can be driven into the cultures of even the most hidebound organizations, reigniting their entrepreneurial fires and infusing them with a renewed sense of purpose and direction.

Why Vision?

Schumpeter's gales of creative destruction are blowing as hard as they ever have.[1] In a world that is shifting so rapidly that the next ten years could witness as much change as the last century, the potential for disruption is high. Meanwhile, a troubling trend is emerging. In 2019, Innosight conducted a survey of executives across a wide variety of industries around the world. Fully 75 percent reported that their planning and forecasting horizons are never more than five years out. Only 10 percent plan for eight to ten years or more.[2]

If you are only thinking two or three years ahead, years five to ten might bring you an unwelcome surprise that you haven't planned for. You could be blindsided by an aggressive challenge from an upstart competitor, putting a ceiling on your growth; a new technology could render your flagship product irrelevant. Worse yet, you might miss a breakthrough opportunity if you don't seize it early on. Most leaders understand this—but the pull of the present prevents them from really engaging with the future.*

Innosight, the strategy and innovation management consultancy that Mark cofounded with Harvard Business School's Clay Christensen, and where Josh is a partner, began with the goal of helping clients harness the theory of disruption that Clay developed and popularized in his seminal book *The Innovator's Dilemma*.[3] (Disruption theory, in a nutshell, proposes that the more successful a company becomes, the more likely it is to fall victim to a new competitor that operates in a new and different way.)

In our early days, we worked with innovation and leadership teams at consumer product giants like Procter & Gamble, leading medical device and pharmaceutical firms such as Johnson &

---

*Of course some industries (biopharma, military contractors, utilities) do have longer horizons, and some (for example, software) have shorter ones. But most organizations need to focus on a longer-term planning horizon than they currently have.

Johnson, great military contractors like Lockheed Martin, and government agencies, such as Singapore's Economic Development Board, to help them gain a better understanding of the disruptions that were threatening them from below and the disruptive innovations they could develop to save themselves. Threats, we showed them, can be turned into opportunities.

But while the teams we worked with had no shortage of good ideas, too many of the initiatives they launched failed to achieve escape velocity and mature into the transformative ventures that they might have become. In some cases, senior management refused to supply them with adequate funding as they launched, or to protect them from their internal rivals as they incubated and scaled; some looked like they were on a path to success but then fizzled. At the root of the problem were the processes by which senior management developed its strategic choices and priorities, which were overdetermined by their existing ways of doing things. As Wendell Weeks, the CEO of Corning, puts it, "It's way easier to hold onto a hill when you're at the top of it than it is to take a hill."[4]

Why is that? In part, it's because of what we call the present-forward fallacy, the seductive notion that an existing business can be extended out in time indefinitely by continuously making improvements to it. Those core improvements, whether incremental or radical, are "sustaining innovations," and they are entirely necessary to keep an organization on track.[5] Every business leader needs to excel in this area and many do. But such improvements are not sufficient to ensure topline growth and sustainability over time. The systematic pursuit of long-term, breakthrough growth is needed as well.

Leaders who think about the future but then focus exclusively on sustaining or efficiency improvements may believe they have a long-term vision and strategy, but often what they have is a glorified operating plan that perpetuates their assumptions about how their markets work today. Even when leaders do understand the

The Four Most Common Failure Modes for Transformative Innovations in Large Organizations

- **Too late.** Leaders recognize the need for new growth but don't commit to it until their competitors have already seized the opportunity.

- **Too few resources.** Leaders appropriately organize and adopt long-term growth initiatives but fail to allocate sufficient dollars, the right people, and enough of their own mindshare to sustain them.

- **Impatience for growth.** Many transformative ventures are slow to bloom. Perhaps an early business experiment fails or has slower than expected results. Instead of redesigning the experiment to learn more, senior leadership pulls the plug. Or maybe it experiences some early-stage success and senior leadership demands that it be scaled up before all of its premises have been thoroughly tested, causing the venture to make a fatal stumble.

- **Competition from the core.** A challenge with growth in the core may cause resources to be diverted away from a promising new venture. Or, in a misguided attempt to restore organizational efficiencies, leadership might "cram" a successful new venture back into the core prematurely, causing it to lose the unique attributes that were responsible for its success.

evolving dynamics of the future and want to change course to embrace them, they often mismanage their responses because they overestimate the riskiness of investments beyond the core. As we'll show, those risks can be managed—and the risk of *not* doing something may be much higher.

Senior leaders' calendars are filled with profit and loss reviews, business plan reviews, marketing reviews, human resources reviews, and so on. Each follows a template, and each is usually concerned with short-term horizons. When they convene as a team, their agendas mostly turn on routine oversight and governance. That is as it should be, when the job at hand is routine management. But when markets shift, consumer preferences change, or new technologies emerge, leaders who solely think in a present-forward way are often caught unawares, busily working to solve today's problems but utterly unprepared for the even bigger ones that are on their way.

This shortsightedness doesn't just afflict businesses. Governments are big organizations too, and they are just as vulnerable to unanticipated change as businesses are. So are universities, great philanthropies, advocacy groups, the military, and even faith institutions. Whether it is the US government's failure to confront the dangers of global climate change or to fix the nation's crumbling infrastructure, universities' inability to gain control of their rising tuitions, religious institutions' struggles to stay connected to their members, or the military's tendency to fight the current war as though it's the last, they all desperately need better ways to plan for and build a more prosperous, equitable, and sustainable future.

In response to these challenges, we've formalized a way of thinking and a set of allied processes that can help leaders think further out than the three to five years that most set as their planning horizon—and find the courage and the wherewithal to create and lead change when it's called for, starting today. *Future-back*, as we call it, is iterative and nonlinear. It's the way of thinking that

The Power of a Long-Term Planning Horizon

- It silences the distracting noise of the here and now, with all its competing demands for attention.

- It allows you to see how faint signals and emerging trends could become fault lines that fracture over time.

- It expands your scope of vision to include beyond-the-core opportunities that will likely take five years or more to incubate and scale.

- It's hard to discuss which of your current efforts may need to be slowed down or stopped. Having a well-developed view of the future takes some of the emotion out of the issue and clarifies what needs to be done today.

- It drives strategic continuity, even as the membership of a leadership team changes over time.

is needed when the objective is to go beyond your organization's established ways of doing things—to help you identify and fill a projected shortfall in a market; reinvent a core business or a flailing function; or develop a disruptive, beyond-the-core product, a breakthrough marketing strategy, or a bold new vision for the enterprise as a whole.

It may sound like a tautology, but the surest way to break free of the barriers to visionary innovation and change is to actually do the hard work of envisioning your future. The fact is, you don't know what you don't know. If you don't think about the future in a systematic way, you won't think about or fully realize the threats and opportunities that await you. Once you begin to see them for yourself, you won't be able to imagine how you could have functioned with such an incomplete perspective.

Lead from the Future

At the highest level, our future-back approach is relatively simple: setting aside your assumptions about the way things work today, think carefully about your destination—your organization's target end state in the future—and then develop and implement a step-by-step plan to get there.

That said, developing and implementing the transformative plans that come out of future-back thinking is anything but easy. The organizational systems and cognitive biases that get in their way don't just go away; they exert a constant, inexorable pressure, and they need to be met with an equal and opposite reaction. Developing successful future-back visions and strategies requires new organizational systems and, indeed, new biases, the most important of which is an abiding belief in your ability to shape the future for the better.

Future-back thinking and planning begins with exploring and envisioning—that is, actively, intensively, and imaginatively immersing yourself in your organization's likely future environment and then determining what you must do to not only fit into that environment but to actively shape it to your needs so you can thrive in it. But it doesn't stop there. We'll show you how to translate your vision into a long-term strategy and then walk it back to the present in the form of concrete initiatives that are programmed and implemented in the right way moving forward, as shown in the figure. While our methods won't allow you to predict the future with absolute certainty (no one can), they will give you the clarity that you need to meet its challenges and opportunities proactively, which,

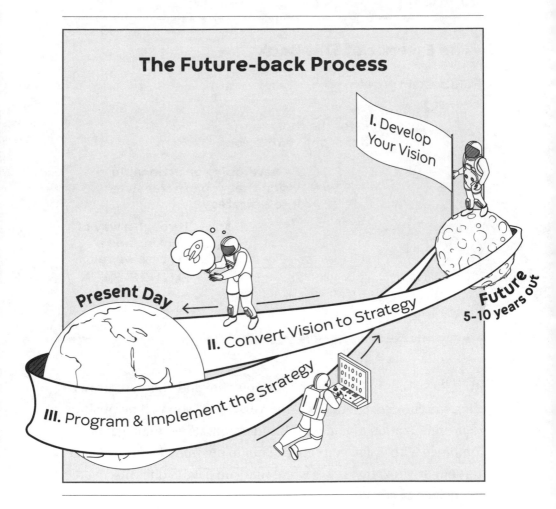

combined with proper planning and disciplined execution, will allow you to better sustain your organization over the long term.

Since senior leaders make the resource allocation decisions that spell the success or failure of breakthrough innovation efforts, they must own them at every phase of their development, working closely with the innovation teams who carry them out on a day-to-day basis. Of course, this doesn't mean you should devote all of your time to the future. Maintaining a healthy and thriving core requires significant leadership attention. In most cases, spending

The Essence of This Book

To sustain growth

Plan for the short term **and** the long term

By developing an actionable vision that you can translate into a strategy

Through a way of thinking and a process we call **FUTURE-BACK**

10 to 20 percent of your time on new, beyond-the-core growth efforts is enough. Spend less, and very likely you will be pushing your organization ahead with blinders on. When management is combined with vision you can lead not to but *from* the future, steering your organization into a world that you have at once discovered and helped to create.

What's Next

Lead from the Future is the capstone of Innosight's thinking about enterprise sustainability and growth as it has developed over the last twenty years. Integrating the disciplines of strategy, innovation, leadership, and culture, it defines and prescribes the principles and practices that allow organizations to truly own their future. In writing it, we have applied both our own ideas and those we have absorbed from other management thinkers, the best practices we have observed in the field, and the attributes of practical visionaries that we have gleaned from our ongoing work with leaders of incumbent businesses. The most successful innovators among them have an innate understanding of the different kinds of thinking that are required under different circumstances and know how to toggle back and forth between them. No management system or tool or leadership development program can replace this critical mindset if it is missing. But the principles that underlie it can be better understood and applied and even institutionalized up to a point.

In part 1, "Principles" (chapters 1 and 2), we define our terms while comparing and contrasting present-forward and future-back thinking, specifying the circumstances that call for each, and describing their applications. We explain what we mean by *vision*—what it is, what it's not (it is emphatically *not* what is captured in the typical corporate vision statement)—and show you how it's different from strategy but nonetheless links to it. Future-back thinking is a mode of learning that is best carried out as teams through what we call strategic dialogues; in using it, you develop a common language and a deep understanding of what your organization can become.

In part 2, "Application" (chapters 3, 4, and 5), we demonstrate how this understanding can be developed and practically applied through our future-back process to develop and implement an organization's long-term vision and strategy.

Part 3, "Making Future-back Repeatable" (chapters 6 and 7), shows you how future-back principles and processes can be permanently embedded in your organization. Chapter 6 presents a new leadership framework that makes the need for future-back thinking among senior teams explicit, and chapter 7 shows how it can be infused into your organization's culture at large via executive development programs, a focus on an organization-wide growth-mindset, and fruitful collaborations with boards of directors.

Finally, in part 4, "Broader Implications" (chapter 8), we consider what other kinds of organizations—governments, the military, universities, even faith institutions—might learn from our future-back principles. In the epilogue, we offer our view of what this all means for twenty-first-century management.

We are not business revolutionaries, and we are not asking you to be one either. But too many of our great organizations are stuck in the present, even as their markets are inexorably shifting away. This book proposes a set of principles to help leaders like you better understand and manage the unique challenges of creating and sustaining beyond-the-core growth, demonstrates them via their successful applications in the real world, and then shows you how you can use them yourself to own the future.

That is what great visionary leaders do. It is what you can do, too.

PART ONE

PRINCIPLES

While virtually every organization began as the brain child of one or more innovative entrepreneurs, even the most groundbreaking tend to become more conservative and set in their ways as they mature, just like people do. Some of that is structural; big organizations can fall captive to their own processes, rules, norms, and metrics, and those of the larger ecosystems that they function in, financial and otherwise.

Much of it has to do with their leaders' mindsets. If you want to change what you're doing, you have to change the way you think. Though present-forward thinking is the necessary and predominant mode for routine, day-to-day business management, visionary leadership demands future-back thinking as well—a different, more generative kind of thinking that is less structured but no less rigorous.

In chapters 1 and 2 we will take a much closer look at both, establishing a set of principles and a common language that we will then demonstrate in the second part of this book.

———————

Chapter 1

THE PERILS OF THE PRESENT-FORWARD FALLACY

Life can only be understood backwards,
but it must be lived forwards.

—Søren Kierkegaard

A string of stage coaches, a horseless carriage, and the Goodyear space tire • When present-forward and when future-back? • The first law of incumbent organizations • The vicious cycle of cognitive biases and organizational incentives • Heating houses by burning the furniture • The tyranny of the urgent • The most reliable predictor of high shareholder returns • The cavalry is not coming

---

Virtually every mature company tries to produce breakthrough innovations, but often what they tout as the wave of the future is just an incremental improvement on what they are already doing—the same old thing, but with a few added bells and whistles, like a coffee-maker that you can operate with your smartphone. Sometimes they do invent something that has the potential to be transformative, but they develop it within a system that is defined and constrained by the facts of the present—like a spaceship in a Jules Verne story with lace curtains hanging over its portholes and a cockpit fitted out with gas lamps, Persian rugs, and overstuffed armchairs.

Have you ever seen a picture of a very early railroad train? The passenger cars looked exactly like stagecoaches, with the good seats inside and the cheap seats on their roofs.

It wasn't much different when the earliest automobiles hit the roads. They looked very much like the horseless carriages that they were, and they were almost as noxious and noisy and uncomfortable to ride in as those early trains. Their passengers knew

c. 1831. Rooftop passengers in the "cheap seats" were usually treated to a face full of smoke and cinders

Source: Science History Images / Alamy Stock Photo.

they were traveling in something novel, but few of them could have realized the extent to which those contraptions would redefine the geography of the future, even as they democratized the privilege of mobility.

The inventors of those early trains and cars weren't thinking about what was to come so much as what already was. They took the transportation concepts of their day, coupled them with new technologies, and projected them out into the world without imagining the array of other developments that were needed for them to achieve their full potential. They exploited those new technologies, but they didn't use them as propellants to new possibilities.

An even more eye-popping example of this is what the Research and Development people at Goodyear's aviation division

c. 1894. The "horseless carriage": one of the first designs for the automobile

Source: Mercedes-Benz Classic.

dreamed up in 1961 for a manned space station. Torus-shaped, with fabric walls that could be folded up flat for the launch and inflated upon deployment, its prototype looked exactly like a giant rubber tire. Needless to say, it didn't get the green light from NASA.

The designers of Salyut, Skylab, and the International Space Station understood that space is an altogether different environment than earth's, so they allowed their functions to determine their forms. Goodyear's R&D people, in contrast, were like the proverbial hammer that sees only nails. When tasked with the creation of something unprecedented, they made a great big tire instead.

Of course, there is nothing wrong with thinking and acting from the present forward when circumstances call for it. It's appropriate when managing an ongoing business, striving for efficiency, improving quality, adding new features to, or otherwise

c. 1961. Goodyear's grand idea for a space station

Source: NASA.

enhancing an existing offering—which describes the majority of managerial challenges. The problem arises when present-forward thinking and processes are employed to address something truly new, unformed, or discontinuous—a breakthrough invention like a passenger train, an automobile, a space station, or a personal computer. To fully leverage the potential of inventions like these, you need to think in a different direction, from the future back.

There are countless business cases about long-established companies that failed because they could not imagine a future in

When to Use Present-forward vs. Future-back

STRATEGY

Present-forward	Future-back
Extend an existing strategy; maintain a linear growth path	Develop a vision and transformative strategy; address a major shortfall or gap

INNOVATION

	Present-forward	Future-back
Outward	Performance Enhancing / Sustaining Innovations	Market Creating Innovations / New Business Models
Inward	Efficiency Innovations / Process Improvement	Cost Transformation / Reinvent the Core
	Sustain	Transform

FOCUS OF INNOVATION

PURPOSE OF INNOVATION

which their core product didn't play a dominant role. Their leaders extrapolated the present forward instead of envisioning a truly different competitive environment. Given the speed of developments with the internet and information technology in general, the computer business is replete with such stories. When the newspaper industry first began to feel the effects of the internet, its present-forward thinkers responded by making a literal PDF replica of the print newspaper and putting it on line. A handful of future-back thinkers, in contrast, recognized how different the digital environment was than print, so they created websites that changed dynamically in real time, and that were hyperlinked, allowing for nonlinear navigation, searching, and the serendipitous discoveries that the web made possible.

To see what can happen when the government applies present-forward thinking to a future-back problem, consider the case of Robert McNamara, the whiz-kid statistician Henry Ford II hired in 1946 to lift his company's bottom line. John F. Kennedy appointed McNamara as his defense secretary in 1961. When the Vietnam War began to heat up during the Johnson administration, McNamara attempted to use the same quantitative methods that had rejuvenated Ford to achieve a military victory. But victory or defeat in war (especially another country's civil war, one that is being fought by unconventional guerilla tactics) is not as easily measurable as success or failure in business.

Instead of evaluating why the Vietcong were fighting and how much each side was willing to sacrifice to achieve their goals; instead of conjuring up a plausible vision of the future and figuring out all the things that would have to be true for the United States to be able to claim victory for itself or for South Vietnam (or what such a victory would even look like), McNamara relied on enemy body counts as his most significant metric of success. But while the United States and South Vietnam consistently stacked up more Vietcong bodies than vice versa, they didn't win the war. A master of execution and operation, McNamara aspired to play the game of war as he knew it more effectively. But his adversary was playing a different game.

At the same time, a future-back thinker who is weak in present-forward execution is no better off than his or her less-visionary peers. Elon Musk, for example, has become a multibillionaire by capturing the imaginations of investors with his futuristic visions of hyperloop transportation systems, high-speed tunnel borers, vertical take-off electric jets, and more. If the United States resumes the exploration of outer space, it will have much to do with SpaceX, the company Musk began in 2002 with a goal of sending people to Mars, and that has pioneered the development of reusable, orbital-grade rockets. As the CEO and guiding spirit of Tesla, Musk has done more to advance battery technology and the commercial viability of electric cars than anyone. But if Tesla is to become more than a high-tech novelty for the well-heeled, it must continue to rise to its present operational challenge of delivering a $35,000 vehicle in high quantities, on schedule, and of a consistent quality. Real progress is being made as we send this book to press, but only time will tell if Tesla fully pulls it off.

The point is, even great visionaries must master the present. Just ask John DeLorean, whose eponymous car company failed to scale, or Dean Kamen, whose Segway, initially touted as an innovation on the scale of the PC and the internet, turned out to be something less.

Why We Get Stuck in the Present

If Newton's first law is the law of inertia, it is also, alas, the first law of incumbent organizations. When they are at rest, they tend to stay at rest. And when they are moving in a certain direction, it requires a great deal of energy and effort to alter their courses. Most incumbent organizations are led by people who are much less future-facing than their founders. As the economist Herbert

Simon postulated in a different context, "Whereas economic man maximizes, selects the best alternative from among all those available to him, his cousin, administrative man, satisfices" (an apt portmanteau of *satisfies* and *suffices*).[1] The managers of big organizations tend to be administrative men and women by definition.

It's not their fault. The business schools they attended inculcated their present-forward approaches; the organizational and financial ecosystems that surround them reinforce them; and the incentive structures that they work within reward them. Bonuses are generally based on the annual results they deliver; even their so-called long-term incentives seldom run any longer than three to five years. Overcoming these barriers to vision requires you to unlearn a lifetime's worth of lessons that taught you to focus on the short term.

Our Ingrained Cognitive Biases

Psychologists and behavioral economists like Daniel Kahneman and Amos Tversky have identified a host of innate cognitive biases that bind us to the present while blinding us to long-term threats and opportunities. Among them are *bounded rationality*, which is our instinct to solve problems based solely on the information that we have immediately at hand. Other cognitive biases are *automaticity*, the ingrained habits borne of doing the same things over and over again; the *availability bias*, which is our tendency to overweigh the data that is the freshest in our minds; the *confirmation bias*, which leads us to interpret data in a way that supports our pre-existing expectations; *loss aversion*, which makes us hate losing money even more than we like to make it; the *sunk cost fallacy*, which compels us to keep wasting money on losing propositions because we've wasted so much on them already; and the *normalcy bias*, which inclines us to overrate the likelihood of things continuing to go as they always have and to discount the possibility of them going horribly wrong. *Hyperbolic discounting* is our tendency to choose a smaller reward that we will receive sooner over a larger reward that we will receive later. There are dozens more of these tendencies and they tend to reinforce each other, working together in vicious cycles that compel us to keep doing what we've always done in the same ways that we've always done them.

Evolutionary psychologists argue that our brains were hard-wired for survival in the Pleistocene epoch, when life was nastier, more brutish, and much shorter than it is today, to paraphrase the philosopher Thomas Hobbes. "Like all animals," Harvard's Dan Gilbert wrote in an *LA Times* op ed some years ago, "people are quick to respond to clear and present danger, which is why it takes us just a few milliseconds to duck when a wayward baseball comes speeding toward our eyes." Despite our evolutionary proclivity for imminent action, humanity has also evolved to anticipate and plan for things that haven't yet happened, which gives us incredible power. But we have to summon up that capability deliberately, making a conscious effort to think both critically and creatively while putting our short-term biases on hold. "The application that allows us to respond to visible baseballs is ancient and reliable," as Gilbert put it, "but the add-on utility that allows us to respond to . . . an unseen future is still in beta testing."[2]

Financial and System Rewards and Incentives

Then there is the dynamic that Clay Christensen defined as "the innovators dilemma."[3] In order to improve their margins and please their best customers, corporations tend to allocate the bulk of their investments toward improvements that sustain, enhance, and make their existing businesses more efficient. New, exciting, and potentially disruptive growth initiatives may get a lot of buzz, but they rarely receive the funding they need. When times are tough and money is tight, they are usually the first to be cut.

In brief, if you want to understand a company's strategy, don't listen to what it says; look at where it spends its money. Disruption tends to start at the low end of the market and only gradually

Roadblocks to Future-mindedness

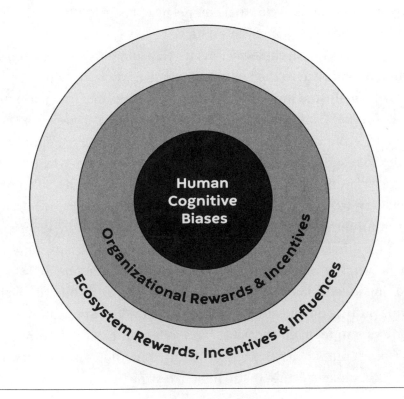

work itself upward; compared to what the core regularly delivers, disruptive products can seem less relevant at first, and hence more dispensable. That said, prioritizing the tried-and-true over the not-yet-known is not foolish or irrational; it's sound management—until it's not, when disruptive developments are reaching full boil. Even then, it is very hard to prioritize the new-and-untried when the old-and-familiar still has some life left in it. Everyone knows that the days of the internal combustion engine are numbered, but if you're running a big car manufacturer, you must sell more of the gas-guzzling SUVs that your customers are still clamoring for. That's why Christensen called it a dilemma. Privileging future-oriented ventures like electric cars over relatively safe ones like SUVs is something of an unnatural act.

So how do you resolve the dilemma? By looking out at a longer-term horizon and judging your present state from the future back. If you define the long-term as three to five years, as most enterprise leaders do, then by definition you are only looking at the present, as both disruption and new ventures take time to develop. Looking out five to ten years (or even more), when the negative effects of disruption are impossible to deny and your new investments will have begun to deliver substantial returns, enhances your ability to balance your short- and long-term priorities and better leverage the art of the possible.

Breakthrough efforts are further disadvantaged relative to mature businesses in defined markets when they are assessed by the kinds of financial metrics that typically guide corporate decision making. Risk-adjusted estimates of profitability for new and untried products can almost never stack up against those for established products because there is so much yet to be learned and discovered. Financial data comes from the past; relying too much on it to make decisions about the future is like looking in the rearview mirror to see where you're going. The only way to override comparative profitability forecasts is with a well-founded judgment that the forecasts are likely wrong because markets will change in fundamental ways.

Leaders naturally worry that investments in altogether new initiatives may starve or even cannibalize their organization's core businesses. Two-time Procter & Gamble CEO A. G. Lafley had some choice words to say about this risk: "Whenever you bring a new product or product improvement to the table in an established business," he told us, "a bright young finance person will raise their hand and say, 'Well, that's going to cannibalize X percent of our business.' But the obvious question that never gets asked is, 'What happens if we don't do it, and competitor A, B, or C does?'" The next question, he said, should always be, "Given the real risks of can-nibalization, what are all the things we can do to minimize its effects?"[4]

A related dynamic that Christensen identified is what he called "the capitalist's dilemma." Since financiers are rightly taught to believe that the efficiency of capital is a virtue, they measure prof-itability not in dollars but as ratios like return on net assets (RONA), return on invested capital (ROIC), and internal rate of re-turn (IRR). But the problem, Christensen wrote, is that "These ra-tios gave investors and managers twice the number of levers to pull to improve their measured performance."[5] Deferring mainte-nance, offshoring workers, and cutting investments in research reduce the denominators, improving the ratios. All of these choices make sense if the aim is to drive up reported profits in the short term, as opposed to ensuring long-term growth and sustainability.

"The only sure way to increase shareholder value," as Roger Martin has noted, "is to raise expectations about the future perfor-mance of the company. Unfortunately, executives simply can't do that indefinitely. Shareholders will look at good results . . . and ratchet up their expectations to the point where managers can't continue to meet them. . . . So the executives invest in short-term strategies, hoping to get out before the inevitable crash."[6]

> **Business leaders are being motivated and rewarded to heat their houses by burning the furniture.**

As much as Wall Street celebrates successful long-term investors like Warren Buffett, the majority of analysts, hedge-fund manag-ers, and institutional investors are looking to place bets that they can collect on right away. Activist investors often reward CEOs who use available cash to buy back shares and punish CEOs who rein-vest it. Plus, as noted above, executives' salaries, bonuses, and incentives are pegged to the short-term profits they deliver. "Most incentive systems are backwards," Scott Cook, the cofounder and leader of Intuit and a member of the boards of P&G and eBay told us in an interview. "They pay for last year's successes. Yet investors invest for a company's future performance."[7]

The Tyranny of the Urgent

Beyond these cognitive biases, organizational rules and norms, and short-term incentives, the senior leaders who make the most important resource allocation decisions are being crushed by what has been called the tyranny of the urgent.[8]

They may admire business visionaries in the abstract, but they typically blanch at the costs in time and mental bandwidth that being one entails. We once worked closely with the CEO of a major American corporation who spent his fifteen-hour days racing from meeting to meeting with his twenty-plus direct reports to put out fires—when he wasn't traveling to plants and branch offices around the world. The only time he had to himself, he told us, was the hour he spent exercising on his treadmill before dawn, which he used to read and answer the emails he hadn't gotten to the day before. He might as well have been on that treadmill all day. His case is hardly unusual. A 2018 report by Michael E. Porter and Nitin Nohria, published in *Harvard Business Review,* analyzed the calendars of twenty-seven CEOs over a full quarter.[9] On average, they had thirty-seven meetings per week, which took up 72 percent of their time.

As overwhelmed by the stresses of the present as they are, where can these over-pressed leaders find the time to think about the future? The stresses of the present are palpable; we feel them in our bodies as we scramble to deal with them, while the threats and opportunities of the future are just ideas. When a pipe bursts in our basement, we rush to call the plumber. When we read about the rising water levels in the oceans, it's easier to push the concern from our minds.

It's dauntingly hard to run a big organization and it gets harder every day. Leaders must set aside time for the future. If that requires them to delegate some of their routine managerial responsibilities to others, then that is what they must do.

Why Long-Term Planning Is Critical

You should always seek out opportunities for beyond-the-core growth, because growth today does not foretoken growth tomorrow, even if you are the most valuable company in the world. As Sandi Peterson, a former vice chairman of Johnson & Johnson who currently sits on the board of Microsoft, put it to us, "People do get lulled into thinking that the future must be fine because they're making their quarters."[10] Even if—*especially* if—you are certain that your organization is on an unstoppable path of multifactorial growth, that growth could easily plateau or plummet if you haven't been building new platforms and opening up new markets, laying the groundwork for a future that is likely to be as different from the present as the present is from the past. When you are thinking solely in the short term, you are by definition blind to both threats (the sudden decline in year six that results from a disruptor's attack) and longer-term opportunities (the sharp spike in revenues that would have come from an initiative that finally started to scale in, let's say, year seven).

Growth is never assured and essential growth, to be clear, is not just financial. There is growth in value and relevance to customers; growth in technological, scientific, and other capabilities; growth in understanding; and growth in organizational wisdom. Absent growth, an organization, like an individual, must be in a state of stagnation or decay.

Efficiency improvements and sustaining innovations may boost your margins for the next few quarters or even the next several

Looking beyond the Horizon

When your planning horizon is just 3 to 5 years, you are blinding yourself to longer-term threats and opportunities

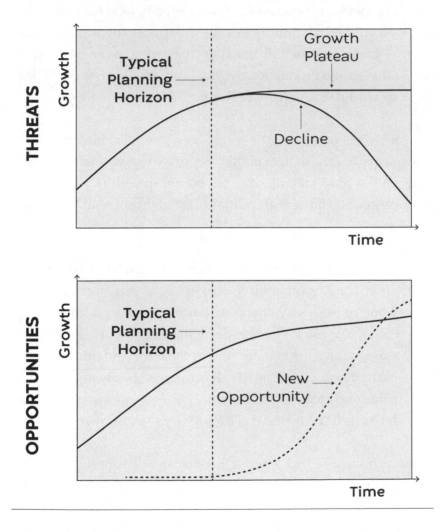

years, but they will not keep you ahead of the curve of long-term change. As Scott Cook put it in our interview with him,

> If you are commoditizing, incremental improvement won't help. The best people and companies do both at the same

time: both execute and look to the future to invent and disrupt. Don't kid yourself, Amazon is a relentless executor
and that's critical to their success. At the same time, they've
created unprecedented industries of the future: cloud
computing (Amazon Web Services), e-books (Kindle), con-
versational computing (Alexa), and more. Toyota too—they
re-invented assembly line manufacturing in the '60s and
'70s (Toyota Production System) and popularized the hybrid
drive. But 99.9 percent of companies focus on today.[11]

Cook's 99.9 percent figure might be hyperbolic, but neither the
prevalence nor the danger of this corporate myopia can be denied.
The only way to stay relevant, Cook continued, is via constant
innovation, and not just at the margins but throughout your whole
enterprise:

How do you drive sustainable growth? You have to think
about innovation in three buckets: First you *improve the
game*, or push it by operating better, but second, you can
change the game, change the business, by figuring out new
ways to leave the competition in the dust. And third, you can
create a new game. The CEO has to drive the org to change the
game and create the next game. It's a personal assessment of
how much you're doing of each. They're all three important.[12]

Even if you are lucky enough to escape disruption, an exclusively incremental present-forward approach is unlikely to create
the long-term growth you need. As the charts on the next page
show, the most reliable predictor of high shareholder returns over
an eight-year-plus period is not the size of your margins, which
don't correlate with long-term share value, but your rate of top-
line growth, which does.

Companies that merely keep pace with the growth rate of the
economy as a whole have a survival advantage that is six to twelve

Long-term Shareholder Return vs. Margin Expansion
No Observable Correlation

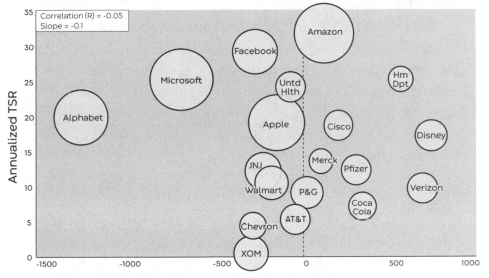

Change in Operating Margin, basis points - Last 8 Fiscal Years

Long-term Shareholder Return vs. Revenue Growth
Strong Correlation

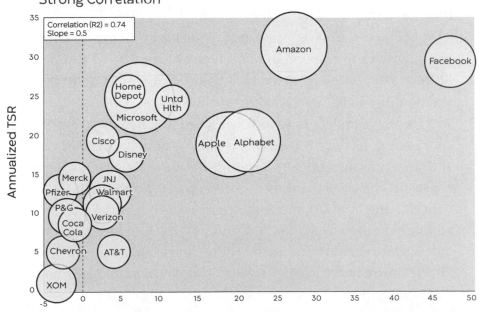

Revenue Compound Annual Growth Rate, % - Last 8 Fiscal Years

Top 20 market cap S&P 500 companies, ex-Financials
Annualized, 8-Year Total Shareholder Return (TSR), 2011-2019
Facebook based on 7 years given May 2012 IPO
Source: Datastream, Refinitiv, S. Patrick Viguerie and John Van Landeghem

◯ Diameter reflects
Latest Fiscal Year Revenue

times that of companies that don't. But to grow faster than the stock market, companies must grow their revenues at a rate that exceeds the GDP.

Privileging risky future-oriented ventures over relatively safe present-forward ones may seem like something of an unnatural act, but no one, least of all us, is telling leaders to mortgage their core businesses and stake everything on an untested vision. The aim is to get as much as you can from your core for as long as you can but at the same time to always be planting seeds you can harvest in the future.

The Cavalry Is Not Coming

Having a powerful vision of the future can go a long way to overcoming all these barriers to long-term, beyond-the-core growth. Really, it may be the only thing that can. The cavalry is not coming: human nature will not change, and the organizational and financial systems that we humans invented will be with us for a long time.[13] But that is not the end of the story.

As bound to the present as we are, we do have that add-on utility that allows us to respond to unseen threats and opportunities. Entrepreneurs often wield it instinctively; if you're in a leadership position in a long-established organization that is biased to the short term, you might have to learn when and how to switch off your present-forward biases, access your future-back capabilities, and use them intentionally. Leading from the future must be a conscious choice, or the present will keep pulling you back.

Just as the innovation teams in great R&D organizations formulate hypotheses and methodically test them to retire risk, senior leaders should continually shape and reshape their vision for the future of their organizations. Think of it as breakthrough R&D for business.

As the next chapter will show, future-back thinking enables you to do just that.

Chapter 2

THINKING FROM THE FUTURE BACK

You can't connect the dots looking forward.
You can only connect them looking backwards.

—Steve Jobs

Apple's digital hub • A clean break from the past and present • The essence of future-back thinking • Thomas Edison's systemic future-back approach • Aetna and "the theory of the business" • Vision vs. strategy • Know-it-alls and learn-it-alls • Attributes of future-back leaders • The learning loop: explore, envision, and discover • Strategic dialogues

---

As an example of what future-back thinking makes possible, we want to revisit the well-known story of Apple's transformation from a niche computer company to the consumer electronics behemoth we know today, driven by its digital hub strategy.

Steve Jobs's incredible leadership abilities—the fabled "reality distortion field" he wielded to help others see what he did and accomplish what they thought was impossible—has been the subject of countless articles, books, and even several big-budget Hollywood movies. Virtually all of them focused on the force of Jobs's outsized personality rather than on the way he systematically articulated and strategically deployed his vision of a radically transformed Apple. No other business case in recent years better illustrates the power of envisioning the future and walking it back to the present.

Jobs, of course, cofounded Apple with Steve Wozniak in 1976 and left the company under a cloud in 1985. When he returned to it in 1997, it had scaled into an enterprise whose core product, the home computer, was beginning to commoditize. The iMac that

Jobs helped develop and launch after he returned was a huge success, but it was still a personal computer that was competing at the high end of a market in which prices were rapidly falling. So, starting in 1999, Jobs began to look forward to 2010, imagining the role that the microprocessor and the personal computer could play in that world and how Apple might prosper in such an environment. In 2000, at an offsite meeting with his top one hundred lieutenants, he further expanded his thinking.

Instead of simply being commodity tools for making spreadsheets, word processing, surfing the internet, and exchanging emails, Apple computers could become the enabling hubs of the whole array of digital devices just coming onto the market—still and movie cameras, music players, DVD players, gaming consoles, ebook readers, and more. The major constraint on the usability of those early devices was their limited power and capacity. They were also jammed with clunky software, making

Steve Jobs Unveiled Apple's Digital Hub Strategy in January 2001

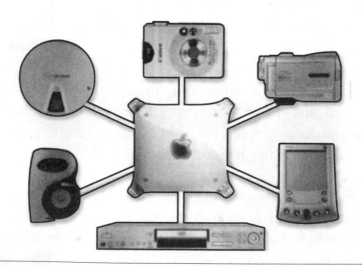

them user-unfriendly. If most of their programming resided on Apple computers instead, they would be easier to operate and could do much more. This could multiply their value by as much as a factor of ten, Jobs said, and ensure that Apple and its computers continued to be commercially relevant.

On the basis of those insights, Jobs announced Apple's new strategy to the world. What he didn't share yet was his bigger and bolder idea—that Apple could be making all those consumer devices itself. Apple didn't have to be just a computer company—it could become a music company, a camera company, a lifestyle company, and even a bricks-and-mortar retailer. Beginning in 2000, Apple began to quietly buy new technologies, set up new and independent teams, and systematically build toward this vision. It had milestone-driven plans for when new products would come online and how they'd build on one another. This vision encompassed Apple's ongoing core business as a computer maker and the digital hub innovation (an adjacent new growth business). It included a plethora of consumer electronics devices Apple ultimately created that transformed whole industries (a set of beyond-the-core moves into its unexplored and underexploited markets, or white spaces).

Wrapping his arms around all those possibilities, Jobs brought them back into the present, one by one. First came the software to power the hub: iPhoto, iMovie, GarageBand, iTunes, and more. Then, in 2001, after a series of strategic acquisitions and an intensive internal development process, Apple debuted the paradigm-changing piece of hardware that would render music CDs and the stores that sold them obsolete. The iPod wasn't the first MP3 player to hit the market, but it held a lot of songs (the tagline of its early ads was "1,000 songs in your pocket"). When the iTunes store opened its virtual doors in 2003, it became by far the easiest MP3 player to fill and use.

Soon Apple was licensing songs from record companies at such a clip that it surpassed them, becoming the largest vendor of recorded music in the world. Now Apple wasn't just selling the digital hub but one of its spokes, along with the content that went into it. More than a breakthrough product, the iPod was a breakthrough business model—a reverse variation on King Gillette's legendary razor handle and blade model, in which songs were sold cheaply to induce customers to buy the much more expensive iPod.

With the advent of the iPhone in 2007, Apple put the rest of the wheel into its customers' pockets. The iPhone was not just a mobile phone, a camera, a PDA, a computer, a music player, a gaming console, and an ebook player in one but yet another breakthrough business model, this one based on the sale of proprietary and third-party apps as well as the phone itself. By the time the iPad was released in 2010, Apple was not only the most valuable technology company in the world; it was on its way to becoming the most valuable company of any kind.

Based on their vision of a different future for home computers, Jobs and his team formulated a strategy to make it a reality and executed it with relentless focus, launching industry-transforming innovation after industry-transforming innovation, growing the value of Apple's market cap from $4.8 billion to $312.6 billion over ten years, an astounding 6,413 percent. And they did it during a decade that began with the bursting of the dot.com bubble and later experienced the most devastating economic crisis in nearly a century.

"You can't connect the dots looking forward," Jobs told Stanford's graduating class of 2005. "You can only connect them looking backwards. So, you have to trust that the dots will somehow connect in your future. You have to trust in something—your gut, destiny, life, karma, whatever."[1] It's a memorable quote, but we don't believe that Jobs and Apple got where they did via fate or "whatever." Whether they do it consciously, following a set of deliberate processes, or instinctively, visionary leaders like Jobs explore the topography of the possible and then, after envisioning how they might master it, walk that vision back to the present and strategically deploy it.

As spectacularly as Jobs's strategy was succeeding, by as early as 2008 he was restlessly looking forward again toward the day when content and data and programming would reside on remote servers instead of in the hard drives of individual computers. In 2010, he laid out his new vision of the future and Apple's place in it for his biographer Walter Isaacson:

> We need to be the company that manages your relationship with the cloud—streams your music and videos from the cloud, stores your pictures and information, and maybe even your medical data. Apple was the first to have the insight about your computer becoming a digital hub . . . and it's worked brilliantly. But over the next few years, the hub is going to move from the computer into the cloud. So, it's the same digital hub strategy, but the hub's in a different place.

"It's important that we make this transition," he added, "because of what Clayton Christensen calls 'the innovator's dilemma,' where people who invent something are usually the last ones to see past it, and we certainly don't want to be left behind."[2]

Jobs died just a year later, and though Apple programs and devices are now thoroughly integrated with the cloud, his second strategy proved less transformative than the first, because Apple's competitors were already going down the same road. Rather than seizing a huge competitive advantage for itself, migrating into the cloud simply kept Apple in the game.

Though the iWatch was developed and launched under Jobs's successor Tim Cook, Cook has mostly defaulted to the present-forward approach of big incumbents, cautiously rolling out "new and improved models" of the iPhone, the Mac, and Apple's other flagship products on a predictable schedule. Some of those improvements (like eliminating the conventional headphone jack from the iPhone 7) may test the limits of customer loyalty, although its brand seems bulletproof for now. Still, as sales of the iPhone plateau internationally, Apple's growth rate has inevitably slowed. That said, Apple's ongoing transition toward services and subscriptions and the $15 billion per year it invests in R&D could slow or even reverse that decline. Apple reportedly has a number of beyond-the-core moonshots in its pipeline, among them an augmented reality headset and a self-driving car. It is likely to need them.

The Essence of Future-back Thinking

Future-back thinkers like Steve Jobs make a clean break from the past and present. Their views of the future are so vivid they are almost tactile and so systemic they interpenetrate their views of the present, determining many of their most important decisions.

Present-forward thinking is high in knowledge and driven by known rules, facts, and data; future-back thinking is low in initial knowledge and high in assumptions—its aim is to discover what *could* be true.

In that respect, it has something in common with the "design thinking" that IDEO's Tim Brown and the business thinker Roger Martin have described.[3] It cannot predict the future, but it can recognize patterns and trends and build on them, fleshing them out with informed imagination to create a plausible picture of how the future might be shaped.

Since present-forward thinkers grapple with what already exists, the logical processes they employ are deductive and inductive, based on known rules as they are applied to or generalized from complete observations. Future-back thinkers, in contrast, employ problem-solving methods that are less structured as they deal with a combination of what is known, what is unknown, and what is imagined or envisioned. To develop their mental models, they use both traditional logic and abductive reasoning, a term coined by the American philosopher Charles Sanders Peirce to describe the thought processes that go into the generation of hypotheses from incomplete observations.

Future-back Thinking Is Systemic

When entrepreneurs and system builders like Cornelius Vanderbilt and Henry Ford looked at the early trains and cars that we described in the last chapter, they didn't see bigger and faster horses. They recognized that such inventions had the potential to completely transform the ways that people traveled and moved goods, giving birth to new industries, infrastructures, and radically changed economies. They envisioned all the new things that would have to be created to support them and all of the old things that would no longer be relevant.

Thomas Edison's approach to electric lighting was similarly systemic. Contrary to popular myth, he didn't invent the incandescent light bulb. The great English chemist Humphry Davy laid the groundwork for it in 1809, with other inventors to follow. Edison didn't start by asking how he could solve the technical problem of making a better lightbulb; that came later. Instead, he asked how he could get consumers to switch from kerosene to electricity. He understood that despite the many advantages of electric light, it would replace kerosene only if it had its own economically competitive network.

So while scores of people worldwide worked on improving the lightbulb, Edison conceived a fully operational system from scratch; one that had never existed before. Its technical platform included generators, meters, transmission lines, and substations, and he mapped out both how they would interact technically and how

Attributes of

Present-forward Thinking

— What is
— Sustaining
— Continuous
— Increments existing paradigm
— Concrete and predictive
— Drive to certainty
— Delivery/managerial
— Linear
— Deductive/inductive
— Analytical
— Facts and data-driven
— Answers
— Build off base
— Point solutions

Attributes of

Future-back Thinking

- What could be
- Transformative
- Discontinuous
- Develops a new paradigm
- Ambiguous and abstract
- Drive to clarity
- Discovery/entrepreneurial
- Multidimensional
- Abductive
- Imaginative and creative
- Assumptions-driven
- Questions
- Clean sheet
- Systems thinking

they would combine in a profitable business. This systems level view led to breakthrough insights. It was widely assumed, for instance, that low-resistance filaments were most appropriate for lightbulbs because they minimized the amount of energy lost as heat. But to make electric light economically competitive with kerosene lamps, Edison determined that he would have to limit the amount of costly copper used in transmission. Thus, he'd need a high enough voltage to maintain current within a narrow wire—and a high-resistance filament in the lightbulb itself.[4] His search for the ideal lamp filament "was conditioned by cost analyses," the science historian Thomas Hughes wrote in the journal *Technology and Culture.* "In his notebooks pages of economic calculation are mixed with pages reporting experimental data, and among these one encounters reasoned explication and hypothesis formulation based on science—the web is seamless. His originality and impact lie . . . in this synthesis."[5]

Edison initially tested his high-voltage/high-resistance system in Lower Manhattan, a favorable foothold market because its buildings were close together and filled with potentially enthusiastic customers—Wall Street firms that worked late into the night and which, not coincidentally, were his potential investors. With J. P. Morgan's financing, he soon controlled an empire of business entities, including the Edison Lamp Company, the Edison Machine Works, and the Edison Electric Light Company. Eventually they merged into the Edison General Electric Company, which was one of the twelve companies that made up the Dow Jones Index when it was first created in 1896.

But if General Electric (GE) began as the creation of a consummate future-back inventor/entrepreneur, it scaled into a conglomerate whose principal focus would be present-forward execution and improvement. Jack Welch, GE's CEO from 1981 to 2001, was a huge exponent and evangelist for Six Sigma, a rigorous process-improvement methodology that consists of five phases: define, measure, analyze, improve, and control. Welch adopted Six Sigma in 1995 and claimed to realize $10 billion in profits from it in its first five years. Like Total Quality Management and Lean Management, Six Sigma is a management method that is focused on what business leaders typically (and rightly) spend the vast majority of their time and mindshare on: honing the existing enterprise rather than evolving or transforming it into something new. But it can't guarantee the future. Many analysts now blame that same present-forward incrementalism, which worked brilliantly until it didn't, for GE's current troubles. When GE was delisted from the Dow Jones Index in 2018, its share price had fallen to $10 and was still rated "very expensive" by J. P. Morgan. As we write these words in the fall of 2019, it is still in the same range.

"The Theory of the Business"

Future-back thinking facilitates the development of a new vision of what a company—or any other kind of organization—can become. The great management theorist Peter Drucker called that "what it can be" the "theory of the business." "Some theories of the business," he wrote more than a quarter century ago, "are so powerful that they last for a long time. But being human artifacts, they don't last forever, and, indeed, today they rarely last for very long at all. Eventually every theory of the business becomes obsolete and then invalid."[6] As GE's leaders can attest, that is even more the case today.

While future-back thinking is more characteristic of entrepreneurs than the professional managers of long-standing enterprises, there are (and have always been) some notable exceptions, among them Mark Bertolini. In 2010, when he became Aetna's CEO, the insurance giant had just completed a banner year in which its net income had soared 38 percent. The passage of the Affordable Care Act (ACA) appeared to hold out still more opportunities for Aetna to prosper, as it would make health insurance available to millions of new customers who hadn't been able to afford it. But when Bertolini looked ahead, the view he saw was much bleaker. Though the ACA had become law, its future was far from assured. And business-as-usual wasn't delivering what the big insurers promised their customers. Having survived a near-fatal skiing accident a few years before and nursed his son through a rare form of cancer, Bertolini had experienced the waste, inefficiency, and poor customer service the system offered firsthand, and he was convinced it had become unsustainable. As he would boldly state in a widely reported speech a few years later in Las Vegas, "The system doesn't work. It's broke today. The end of insurance companies, the way we've run the business in the past, is here."[7]

Fortunately, Bertolini also conceived a more hopeful view of what Aetna could become. Unfettered by its past or present, he imagined how the company could flourish—and beyond that, how it could change the world for the better. To make that vision a reality, Aetna's mission became "building a healthier world—one person, one community at a time." Henceforth, Bertolini told his board, Aetna would focus on ensuring its customers easy access to high-quality, affordable healthcare, that their healthcare experience became simpler and more responsive, and that their health improved as a result (which would lower Aetna's costs).

For years, Aetna operated primarily as a business-to-business company that treated the benefit managers at the large- and medium-sized corporations that purchased the bulk of its policies as its primary customers. The policies offered members access to a broad network of healthcare providers that delivered sick care and some wellness and prevention services. Those policies however, were becoming increasingly unaffordable for both employers and individual policyholders, who were accounting for a growing share of the market, and the outcomes they delivered were often poor. Putting in place more complicated claim payment services aimed at reducing waste and inefficiency only made the experience more complex and unappealing for members. Negotiating lower rates with providers proved insufficient to address the challenge of affordability. Aetna, Bertolini realized, needed to go to the source of the problem—the choices consumers make on a day-to-day basis that dramatically influence their health and therefore the cost of insuring them. To make healthcare affordable, and the healthcare experience simple and responsive, Aetna would have to actively partner with consumers to improve their health.

Now a part of CVS Health, Aetna has transformed itself into a consumer-centric company focused not just on the delivery of healthcare but also on health. "We know that healthcare is personal, and that's why the people we serve drive every decision we make. We are focused on them, their communities, and all the factors that affect their overall well-being," its new mission statement declares.[8]

Being able to see when it's time for an organization "to reenergize, renew, reframe, and rethink [its] purpose," as Microsoft CEO Satya Nadella (another future-back enterprise leader) puts it (and it is *always* that time in some part of an enterprise, if it's big and complicated enough), is one part of what it means to be a visionary leader.[9] The other is having a fully developed, fully actionable idea of what that new theory of the business should be—and a concrete plan to bring it into being.

Edison's dream of an electric system that would be so efficient and inexpensive that "none but the extravagant would burn tallow candles"[10] was an entrepreneur's vision of a future that he and his organization would build from the ground up. Mark Bertolini built out his vision of an Aetna that would lower patients' costs while improving their health outcomes by working within and beyond his company's existing core. More than the vaguely inspiring aspirations that are conveyed by a traditional corporate vision statement (*to be the best in our category*), actionable visions are concrete enough to grab hold of and feasible enough that they

Vision vs. Strategy

It's not just the what of a vision that is important but the future-back mental processes that leaders use to develop one. Steve Jobs's vision of the digital hub was enabled by a way of thinking that allowed him to reframe not only Apple's strategy but its very identity.

How might leaders of organizations of all kinds harness this kind of thinking? To answer that question, we must understand what exactly we mean by *vision*, and how it's different than *strategy*.

The online *Macmillan Dictionary* defines vision as the ability to "think about or plan for the future, using intelligence and imagination"; an "idea or hope of how something should be done, or how it will be in the future"; and simply the "ability to see."[11] When we use it in a business context, it encompasses all of those meanings, but what we mean specifically *is having a clear point of view on the markets of the future and the role that your organization can play in that new and different world*. Having a really powerful vision can unleash the potential to transform whole industries.

When we call a business leader a visionary, we mean they have a vivid, systems-level understanding of their organization's best possible future. But an inspiring and galvanizing vision is only the "what," not the "how." Vision is made actionable through strategy, which is the means to achieve it.

VISION	vs.	STRATEGY
Choices made about the long-term future (five- plus years out)		Choices made in the near term (one- to three- year horizon)
Can define a "new game to play"		Determines how to win the existing game or the new game that is defined
Defines the ends/ the destination		Defines the means/the journey to get there
Inspires the organization		Operationalizes the vision or improves the ability to win the existing game

Simply put, strategy is a way to win a game. Vision tells you what game you will play. The two go together, as vision without strategy is inspiration without a real way to get to action.

can be built out strategically, though they must be continually revised and fine-tuned in the light of the feedback they produce as they come into contact with reality.

The Leader as Learner

Whether they self-identify as a future-back visionary or a present-forward doer, every leader has the potential to see farther and clearer than he or she thinks they can, provided they are willing to learn new things and unlearn old ones.

In his book *Hit Reset*, Nadella[12] describes how Carol Dweck's book *Mindset*, which Nadella had read on his wife's recommendation to gain a better understanding of his daughter's struggles in school, opened his eyes to a fundamental problem with Microsoft's culture.[13] Dweck had identified two kinds of students: "know-it-alls" and "learn-it-alls." Know-it-alls are smart but reluctant to stretch or challenge themselves lest they lose face with their peers or superiors, or worse still, find out they aren't as smart as they think they are. Learn-it-alls, in contrast, accept it as a given that they don't know all there is to know. While know-it-alls compete with and undercut their peers, learn-it-alls collaborate with them. While know-it-alls stick to platforms they thoroughly understand, learn-it-alls develop new ones. Microsoft, Nadella realized, had become a culture of know-it-alls who were avoiding the most difficult problems, foreclosing the possibility of true discovery. If the company was ever to regain its innovative edge, he wrote, it would have to become a culture of learn-it-alls. Future-back thinking requires a culture like this to succeed, and it starts with its leaders.

Both present-forward and future-back processes entail the acquisition and application of knowledge, but while present-forward processes use data linearly and more mechanistically

The Attributes of Future-back Leaders

There are a lot of good books that zero in on the key attributes of successful leaders, among them Warren Bennis's classic *On Becoming A Leader*.[14] Bennis stressed the "contagious optimism" that allows leaders to rally others around their visions, their eye for talent, and the integrity that fosters trust. Future-back leaders must have all of those virtues, of course, but what distinguishes them most is their capacity for learning. They are curious about everything and, in the spirit of the ancient philosopher Socrates, they also know what they *don't* know. They are humble and good listeners (because it helps them to learn) and good stewards, in that they put their organizations' long-term interests above their own. They are comfortable with ambiguity, able to make connections and recognize patterns in noise, and willing to go beyond facts and work off of hypotheticals if that will bring them closer to what they need to know.

Future-back leaders are oriented to the big picture but attentive to its individual pixels. They are decisive when they need to be, but patient to find the best solutions—and willing to iterate for as long as necessary to do so. Importantly, they are also skilled communicators and storytellers, which is how they convince their own people and other constituents to embrace their envisioned future. Above all, they are flexible and adaptable, willing to continually adjust and reshape their visions in light of what they learn as they work with their teams to translate them into reality.

The Learning Loop
Future-back thinking is refined through a process of iterative learning

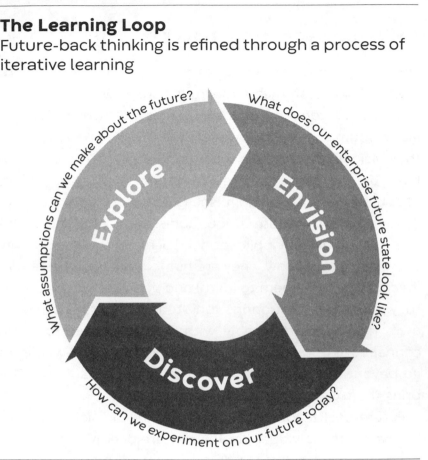

(collect it, parse it, apply an algorithm, and execute), future-back processes entail a learning mode that is, to borrow an insight from Socrates, more akin to the kindling of a flame than the filling of a vessel. Geared to *exploration, envisioning,* and *discovery,* it can be depicted graphically as a generative loop, as seen in the diagram.

Having defined the scope of an opportunity or a problem to be solved, knowledge and insights are developed in the exploration phase of the loop. Then a solution to the problem or a new idea or innovation to address the opportunity is envisioned. In the discovery phase, the solution, new idea, or innovation is tested in order to determine its viability. The learning that emerges from the testing is then used to develop still more questions, which yield deeper insights as the cycle of exploring, envisioning, and testing continues. With each turn through the loop, the idea or solution matures and becomes better understood and further fleshed out.

To illustrate the process, consider the basic steps of developing a new business or venture effort. First, you work to define what needs to be learned. Then you explore the future market opportunity you are trying to develop. You collect as much information as you can about the future market and develop assumptions about the consumer, technology, and other needs you will have to address. Then you envision a new business model or system that addresses all those assumptions. In order to discover a viable model that actually works in the market, you test your business model design in a pilot market, much like Thomas Edison did when he demonstrated his electrical system in downtown Manhattan. Armed with the insights you have gleaned from your test and learn effort, you then revisit "explore" to seek out new things to be learned and further insights and knowledge that will need to be developed. Then you revisit "envision" to adjust the business design and retest it in market to discover still more, turning your assumptions into knowledge. This learning loop is foundational to our future-back vision and strategy development process, which we will introduce to you in part 2, the "Application" section of this book.

Strategic Dialogues

The learning loop is best enabled through strategic dialogues—structured conversations in which leaders work through their ideas as a team, diverging and ultimately converging on key questions and assumptions. Often they are facilitated to encourage the kind of iterative, free-floating thinking that is needed, while at the same time keeping the discussion on track (you will read more about this in the pages to come).

> Unstructured problem solving is necessarily messy and is best carried out collaboratively as a team, bringing a multiplicity of perspectives, skills, and knowledge to bear.

While the members of the team may or may not be visionary as individuals, if they are at once diverse in their capabilities, experiences, and cognitive styles, and disciplined enough that they can ultimately agree to speak in one voice, they can develop a shared language, vocabulary, and perspective, and a rich, multidimensional point-of-view. As the organizational behavioralist Frank Friedlander put it, "Differences must come into close contact for learning to occur."[15] What matters most is:

- **Who's at the table.** The participants must include the people who make the resource allocation decisions that determine the success or failure of the new strategies and initiatives, plus a few key people who have special knowledge of relevant subject matter (perhaps the R&D executive who is responsible for the technology in question, or a key regional leader). The *who* is a matter of judgment; what's critical is that there are not so many people that all their voices can't be heard. Typically, that limits the group to at least five and at most fifteen participants.

- **The ground rules.** The discussion is guided by the future-back tenets we have described thus far, meaning that the focus is on what *could* be as opposed to what *is*. The purpose of the dialogues is as much to explore, imagine, and learn as to prove, confirm, or solidly decide. That means things can't be rushed; these dialogues are very different than the typical two-hour strategy review, which frequently devolves into a race to get through a sixty-page PowerPoint deck.

- **The process.** Aided by the facilitators, the leaders work iteratively to: (1) Get to the right questions, (2) diverge and then converge on the right set of assumptions, and (3) use those assumptions to hone in on the right choices. Innovative techniques can be deployed to generate the right mindset for these conversations. We will describe a few in a later chapter; some of our Innosight colleagues have shared theirs in *Harvard Business Review*.[16]

Future-back Thinking as Applied to Business Processes

There are established processes in big organizations, both within particular functions and cutting across them, that line up as future-back. We briefly describe some of them below, while comparing them to their present-forward counterparts.

Finance and Accounting
Annual Budgeting vs. Zero-Based Budgeting

Budgeting for an existing business is typically built off an established base and updated by projecting current circumstances forward. Zero-based budgeting discards the base, building a budget that is based purely on what is envisioned being needed. Budgeting for new beyond-the-core initiatives should be zero-based so as not to force an emergent round peg into an existing square hole.

Marketing
Needs-Based Market Research vs. Jobs to Be Done Market Research

Needs-based market research looks to fill gaps in customers' needs and wants specific to an existing product or service so they can be satisfied via incremental improvements to them. But as Peter Drucker said, "The customer rarely buys what the company thinks it is selling him."[17]

Jobs to be done market research spreads the net much wider by asking consumers open-ended questions about what they are trying to get done or what progress they are trying to make in their lives. By posing questions in this way, researchers are more likely to surface consumers' deepest desires. "Your customer is unlikely to give you the disruptive idea because if they could, they wouldn't need you," says Corning's Wendell Weeks. "What they can do is identify their pain. Customers are really good at understanding it, but they don't always know how to solve their pain. You should listen to the problem and then engage the right people to figure out how to solve it."[18] (See the sidebar for more on jobs to be done.)

Innovation Teams
Platform-Based Planning vs. Discovery-Driven Planning

Writing in *Harvard Business Review* in 1995, Rita McGrath and Ian MacMillan contrasted conventional platform-based planning, which, as they put it, "operates on the premise that managers can extrapolate future results from a well-understood and predictable platform of past experience," with discovery-driven planning, which acknowledges that "at the start of a new venture, little is known and much is assumed." Platform-based planning proceeds from present-forward thinking; discovery-driven planning is future-back, because, as McGrath and MacMillan wrote, it "systematically converts assumptions into knowledge as a strategic venture unfolds. When new data are uncovered, they are incorporated into the evolving plan. The real potential of the venture is discovered as it is developed."[19]

A product development effort that is based on the core platform can be evolved and rolled out in a traditional stage or phase gate process (scoping, building a business case, development, testing and validation, launch). A beyond-the-core initiative, in contrast, may require reaching outside the enterprise to acquire new capabilities and business models. As it is developed and implemented, teams must leave room for serendipity, late learning, and strategic pivots.

Strategy
Typical Strategic Planning vs. Future-back Vision and Strategy Development

Traditional strategic planning is highly data-driven and analytic; it has evolved to be almost like budgeting, as it uses a company's present financial circumstances as a base or template and then extends it into the future. Much of the work is carried out by staff rather than senior leaders themselves.

In contrast, future-back vision and strategy comes out of a process of active learning via structured dialogues, as leaders work together in a much more participative way to build a shared understanding of a very different future and align on it. It's more organic; participants focus on the questions as much as the answers, on assumptions as much as facts.

———————————

Jobs to Be Done

Jobs to be done theory was first popularized by Clayton Christensen in his 2003 book, *The Innovator's Solution*.[20] Framing purchase decisions in terms of what a customer is trying to accomplish rather than their preference for one product feature over another allows you to think outside the box of your existing offerings and zero in on what might motivate a customer to buy a different and better solution (Clay famously illustrated this idea with an aphorism attributed to the longtime Harvard marketing professor Ted Levitt: "No one goes to the hardware store to buy a quarter-inch drill; you go to buy a quarter-inch hole.") Thinking in terms of jobs rather than products gives you insights into not just your potential customers but your real competition in the future (and not just in your product category but in whole other industries as well, which might offer better solutions for your customer).

As Christensen and colleagues wrote in their recent book *Competing against Luck*, successful innovations "perform jobs that formerly had only inadequate or nonexistent solutions"—or that weren't even recognized as needs until they were met.[21]

There are functional jobs (getting better gas mileage, for example), social jobs (wanting to be perceived as more energetic and confident than you might feel), and emotional jobs (wanting to feel like you're a better spouse or parent) that businesses need to understand and respond to. Frequently, more than one job is relevant, which means that you must know how to prioritize them in terms of their degree of importance and the level of satisfaction that they provide. It's also important to remember that the job to be done framework applies not just to your potential customers but to other stakeholders as well. Airbnb and Uber, for example, fulfill critical jobs on both the supply and the demand ends of their industries—allowing car and home owners to monetize their currently unproductive assets by giving people rides or renting space, while offering people who need to rent transportation or temporary accommodations a digitally accessible (and often cheaper) alternative to traditional taxis and car services and hotels. Another classic example of this is in healthcare, where the jobs to be done of payors, providers, and various regulatory bodies weigh as heavily as the patients' jobs to be done.

Focusing on your customers' future circumstances and jobs—as opposed to building off of your existing products' features or your customers' stated needs of today—gives you a better way to understand your opportunities. This is why a jobs-to-be-done approach is foundational for the design of future-back strategies, as you will see in chapter 3.

In the next three chapters, we will take you through our future-back vision and strategy development process, starting with a blank sheet of paper and ending with a set of concrete business initiatives. As you will see, vision and strategy development is never a one-and-done; leaders must revisit and reshape it continually as their assumptions are tested against reality.

PART TWO

APPLICATION

We've talked about the what and the why of vision and argued that a future-back way of thinking will allow you to tap into its power. Next, we'll show you how you can apply it to the development and implementation of a long-term strategy. But first, we want to tell you a story about a leader whose vision was truly inspiring, but who needed a way to bring it to life in a big, complex organization.

A Vision for the Future of Healthcare

William N. Hait peered into the future and saw a different and better way to practice medicine. He consistently and eloquently communicated that vision to his teams, and they shared his excitement about it. But then they would go back to their offices and laboratories and do the same things that they always had, pursuing the same projects in the same ways.

Dr. Hait was the global head of R&D at Janssen, the pharmaceutical division of Johnson & Johnson. He commanded a budget of roughly $7 billion and led thousands of scientists around the world. With his visionary boss Dr. Paul Stoffels, J&J's chief scientific officer, he and his colleagues oversaw a renaissance in productivity that led to the development of thirteen new drugs launched between 2011 and 2017 that generated over $50 billion in cumulative revenue in the 2011–2018 timeframe. Many of those drugs were transformative in their impacts, redefining the standard of care for devastating diseases like prostate cancer and multidrug-resistant tuberculosis. But as well as things were going for Janssen, it wasn't enough for Hait.

"I always tell my teams—quoting John F. Kennedy—that the best time to fix the roof is when the sun is shining," Hait says. "With our success I felt we had earned the right to think beyond the present."[1] Looking forward, Hait saw a clear need and a tremendous opportunity.

> When I was practicing as an oncologist, patients always asked me the same heartbreaking question—"What could I have done to avoid getting cancer? Could I have prevented this?" The stark reality you face is that too many of your patients die. With some cancers, nearly all of them do. Most of our existing treatments are designed to keep things under relative control for as long as possible, but for too many patients, that isn't very long at all. When we have a new therapy, we sometimes get excited about Kaplan-Meier curves that demonstrate improved survival rates of only several months. As a doctor, I'd always wondered why we couldn't do a better job of preventing cancer from happening in the first place, or intercepting a cancer-causing process. Then, when I got to Janssen, I saw that a similar pattern held for other diseases, like Alzheimer's, diabetes, and auto-immune disorders. Our treatment paradigm is so limited. In the future, people will look back and consider it primitive that we waited until we were diagnosed with a disease before we did something about it. As a leader at a major global healthcare company, I wanted to use my platform not just to predict what could come to be in time, but to make it happen as fast as possible.

Hait gives the example of colorectal cancer. In its advanced state, cancer cells mutate rapidly, outpacing the therapies with which doctors attempt to control them. Patients suffer, the drugs and surgeries are enormously expensive, and mortality rates are extremely high. But every colon cancer begins as a polyp that can be snipped out in a matter of seconds during a routine colonoscopy. The fundamental problem, then, is less *how* colorectal cancer is treated than *when*. If it were possible to intervene earlier, when disease-causing processes are just beginning, outcomes would be much better.

The same pattern plays out with other diseases. Heart attacks and strokes ravaged developed countries for decades; treating high cholesterol with statins well before a heart attack or other advanced cardiovascular event occurs changed that. Hip fractures can be a death sentence for the elderly; strengthening bones with proactive osteoporosis therapies can prevent them. Scientists also suspect that the best time to treat Alzheimer's disease is before cognitive symptoms appear; once memory loss becomes apparent it may be too late to significantly alter its course.

Still, the dominant mode in our healthcare system is "break/ fix"—something breaks, and doctors rally to fix it. This is a matter of practicality, as scarce resources are triaged to solve the most acute problems. But it's also a relic of an era when we knew very little about the underlying mechanisms that cause disease. Biological understanding has increased exponentially in recent years, presenting new possibilities.

"In the not too distant future," Hait predicts, "each of us will know the diseases to which we are susceptible. An ecosystem of passive biosensors and trackers—like the step-counters on our smartphones—will monitor our biometric signals, and the equivalent of a check engine light will turn on when something inside of us begins to go 'out of spec.' In many cases we won't be sick yet—but we will be at risk. Society will demand new types of solutions to address these risks, and the company that creates them will be the next Johnson & Johnson.

"We're already Johnson & Johnson, so why shouldn't it be us?" Hait challenged his teams. "J&J is the biggest, arguably most innovative healthcare company in the world. If we trained our awesome firepower on intercepting disease with targeted investments in the health products that will define the future, it would not only change the way that medicine is practiced—it would drive breakthrough growth for our company."[2]

Everyone at Janssen could see the incredible promise of disease interception—but when push came to shove, they hesitated. Again and again, when Janssen's investment plans were drawn up, the programs that received the most funding were the ones that were focused on strengthening and extending its current positions.

It wasn't that Hait's colleagues didn't believe in the mid- to long-term-oriented business ideas that emerged from his vision— Janssen's is a drug discovery and development business after all, where all new ideas are risky and long-term oriented. The problem was the ideas didn't fit neatly into established industry business models and therefore carried new, unknown, and hard-to-quantify risks. How can you ascribe value to something that *prevents* a disease from happening rather than cures it when it does? They didn't always have benchmarks to estimate pricing or established regulatory paths to follow. In many cases, they'd require new capabilities that stretched beyond the boundaries of the pharmaceutical business, like tools and techniques to identify risk and encourage behavior change. In short, Hait's vision was potentially disruptive to the core business, and a core business that is as established and well-run as Janssen's instinctively rejects potential disruptions. Its systems are designed to stamp out variation and limit risk.

In 2016, Hait realized that a vision alone wasn't enough; he'd have to reprogram the management system through which Janssen organized and allocated its resources. To do that, he needed a method to translate his personal vision into a powerful vision for the organization and then convert it to an implementable

The Future-back Process

Informed by principles derived from our work on transformational growth and innovation strategies with leadership teams at many dozens of large organizations and our study of the intuitive habits of visionary leaders, our future-back process is designed to help leaders develop visionary strategies and bring them to life

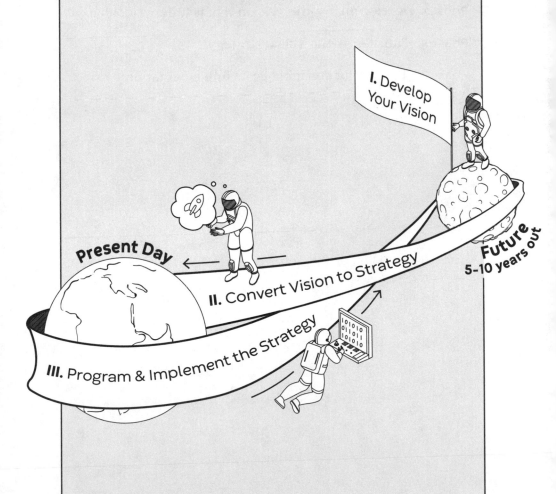

I. Develop Your Vision

Present Day

Future 5-10 years out

II. Convert Vision to Strategy

III. Program & Implement the Strategy

strategy—one others could see, understand, embrace, and systematically bring to life.

Informed by principles derived from our work on transformational growth and innovation strategies with leadership teams at many dozens of large organizations, and from our study of the intuitive habits of visionary leaders, our future-back methods are designed to help leaders develop visionary strategies and bring them to life.

As the graphic shows, the future-back process unfolds in three major phases, which are described in chapters 3, 4, and 5:

Phase I: Develop an inspiring vision that is fully actionable

Phase II: Translate it into a clear strategy

Phase III: Prepare for and manage its implementation

_____

Chapter 3

CREATING AN INSPIRING AND ACTIONABLE VISION

The future cannot be predicted,
but futures can be invented.

—Dennis Gabor

Industry inflection points • Jobs to be done of the future • View of the world statements • An impressionist painting, not a photograph • Four archetypal implications for your future • Vision as aspiration and purpose • Strategic narratives

---

Future-back work begins with a series of structured dialogues in which senior leaders develop a compelling long-term vision or add definition to one that is already conceived but is meeting organizational resistance (as with William Hait's). That said, future-back should never be thought of as a rote process with checklists and prescribed timelines. The phases we outline are more organic and flexible; you should work through their principles in the manner that is best suited for your organization and its strategic challenges.

Your first task is to explore what the future is likely to hold, targeting the right time horizon. Then, you grapple with the implications of that future for your organization, developing a high-level view of what your customers will value and how market dynamics will work, characterizing the major threats and opportunities that are likely to emerge, and assessing where business-as-usual would likely lead. Finally, you assert a point of view on how to best respond to and shape that future, defining the desired future state of your enterprise inclusive of both the

Phase I: Develop Your Vision

Step 1: Paint a picture of the future environment

- Target time horizon
- Jobs to be done of the future
- View of the world statements

Step 2: Identify major implications of the future

- Four archetypal implications
- Confronting the future head-on

Step 3: Envision the future state of your business

- Core, adjacent, and new growth
- Aspirations and purpose
- Strategic narrative

I. Develop Your Vision

Present Day

II. Convert Vision to Strategy

Future 5-10 years out

III. Program & Implement the Strategy

evolution of its current businesses and the development of new ones. Put it all together and you've got a vision that's ready to be translated into a future-back strategy.

Now, let's take a closer look at each of the steps that make up this first phase.

Step 1: Paint a Picture of the Future Environment

Imagine the leadership team of AT&T convening in 1980 to address the rise of wireless communications, or a newspaper company in 2000 contemplating the impact of a future in which news will be available online anywhere, anytime—and classified ads will be free. This is the type of discussion you should start with, and to do so you need to hone in on the right time horizon.

Specify a Time Horizon and Its Inflection Points

Identify the potential inflection points in your industry and focus on the timeframe when they are likely to occur—when new paradigms will mature to the point of significance and new technologies will converge to open up both potential disruptions and new opportunities. Consider the emerging fault lines in and around your industry, the early signals of upheaval and potential disruption. Perhaps your customers' needs are shifting or low-cost competitors are emerging. When might these trends begin to tip?

Even if you don't expect a dramatic phase change in the years ahead, we suggest pushing beyond your typical planning and forecasting horizons to a point where business as usual won't guarantee results, and the current trajectories of your markets are no longer certain. A defense contractor selling fifteen-year programs should look out twenty years or more. Conversely, an app development company operating at the speed of the

Industry Inflection Points

The table below outlines examples of inflection points in major industries—specifically, the years that the disruptive trends in the center column can be expected to mature to a point where they will have business significance. The dates, of course, are simply informed estimates, but they can help guide your discussions about your future state.

Industry	Disruptive Trend	Timeframe
Automotive	Autonomous vehicles	2030
Energy	At-scale storage	2030
Entertainment	E-sports	2022
Healthcare	Fee-for-value payment models	2025
Professional & Legal Services	Automation of key tasks	2025
Life Sciences	Gene and cell therapies	2030
Media	Virtual and augmented reality	2027
Medtech	Robotics and digital surgery	2030
Restaurants	Delivery on demand	2022

internet should look out no more than five years or so for the next architectural shift.

> **The key is to focus on a date that is distant enough to stretch your thinking, but not so far-off that it is utterly unrelatable.**

In 2016, William Hait and the Janssen team looked out to 2030, several years past the time horizons of their traditional drug development plans, zeroing in on four major shifts in the medical and life sciences ecosystem they expected to accelerate as new technologies and new biological understanding unlock new possibilities:

1. Life Sciences R&D will change its focus from understanding the manifestations of disease to understanding its underlying mechanisms, processes, and risk factors.

2. Disease diagnosis will shift from a reactive mode at the point of clinical manifestation to personalized, precision prognostics, with continuous surveillance of at-risk patients to detect incubating diseases before the onset of symptoms.

3. Therapies will shift from one-size-fits-all treatments and management plans to personalized, integrated interventions that combine multiple modalities, from behavioral to biologic.

4. Healthcare delivery models will shift from fee-for-service to fee-for-value and from traditional providers to integrated networks of in-person and virtual care settings.

None of these trends on their own were surprising; each was already apparent in various corners of the marketplace. That is

Emerging Fault Lines

Key Diagnostic Questions

Customer needs:

Do customers we don't currently serve have emerging unmet needs? If so, does that signal an opportunity that a new competitor could seize?

Are our customers loyal to our product, or are they captive for lack of other options? Would they defect if they could?

Could emerging technology simplify how end users' needs are met?

Performance metrics:

Will the customers of tomorrow define quality differently from the way today's customers do?

How closely do our customer satisfaction and financial metrics correlate? Are our customer satisfaction scores as strong as our financial indicators?

Do our products or services have more features or complexity than most of our customers value?

Is there a new metric that aligns with the needs of future customers?

Industry position:

Is a disruptive technology emerging that could significantly change the cost-value equation in a major part of our industry?

Are our customers starting to bring our services in-house or to outsource them to someone else?

Is our industry expanding to include new kinds of competitors? Is there consolidation among major players—signaling that it's becoming harder to make money in the traditional way?

Business model:

Is at least one emerging competitor in our industry following a different business model—even if at the moment that model looks financially unattractive?

Is the way we make money aligned with how value is created for customers? Are customers balking at price increases or added fees?

Will the strategic assumptions that underlie our existing model—assumptions about risk, differentiation, and growth—hold true as our industry changes?

Talent and capabilities:

Will we be fulfilling customer needs that require new skills to be brought on board?

Have our company and industry struggled to attract tech-savvy talent?"

not unusual. As the science fiction writer William Gibson put it, "the future is already here; it's just not very evenly distributed."[1] The power of the analysis came from thinking carefully about a world in which those trends worked together to create a new normal.

Focus on the Jobs to Be Done of the Future—and How to Solve Them

Once you've determined the time horizon you're targeting and the major trends that will shape it, describe what you expect will be happening in and around your relevant markets. What are the circumstances you think your current and targeted customers might be in given the confluence of relevant trends? As technologies mature, new ones emerge, and business models evolve, which of today's jobs to be done (as described in chapter 2) will be increasingly satisfied (or not)—and, consequently, what new issues will arise, presenting new and valuable opportunities?

One example the Janssen team wrestled with: there are massive markets for direct-to-consumer health solutions (such as herbal supplements) that are lightly regulated and have little or no clinical data to support their efficacy claims. But many people buy them hoping they will help ward off disease, reflecting a deep underlying job to be done. While they usually don't have much clinical effect, most are relatively harmless and widely accessible. Many disease interception solutions will have to be similarly safe and accessible, since they'll target people who are not yet sick. The opportunity lies in designing direct-to-consumer solutions that work repeatably and reliably, and developing the evidence to prove it.

Focusing on the jobs to be done of the future led to strategic clarity for the leadership team of a diabetes management company in 2012 and 2013. Their main product line, blood glucose meters, partially met patients' underlying job to be done of managing their diabetes by providing a nearly instantaneous glucose reading from a drop of blood. But, after two decades of robust growth, the category was beginning to commoditize as competitors offered comparable devices at lower price points. Meanwhile, as the diabetes epidemic continued to mount, diabetes-related costs to private payors and health systems rose too, creating a conflict with their own driving job to be done, which is controlling costs. What's more, emerging technologies such as continuous glucose monitors (small implants that automatically and continually track blood sugar) and digitally enabled diabetes management services promised to address patients' underlying job to be done more effectively. They weren't ready yet, but all indications suggested they would be in the next five to ten years.

Focusing on the jobs to be done of the future, the management team concluded that payors would increasingly steer patients to their competitors' less expensive blood glucose meters. New products based on new technologies that better addressed patients' needs would command premium prices from those same payors, further exacerbating the challenge to their existing business. The leaders resolved to devise a strategy to bridge from their current products to the new solutions before it was too late.

The leadership of a major automotive company had a similar epiphany in 2016. Cars are such an important part of our lives because of all the jobs to be done that they satisfy. There are functional jobs to be done, like simply getting from point A to point B— commuting to work, for example. There are more circumstantial jobs to be done, like occasionally needing to haul furniture. And then there are pure *social* and *emotional* jobs to be done, like wanting to impress your peers or knowing the car your teenager drives to school is safe. In the past, most Western families solved those jobs by owning a couple of vehicles—perhaps a sporty sedan for one parent to commute in and a minivan or an SUV to chauffeur the kids and fill with luggage when going on vacation.

But change was on the horizon. As the automotive executives contemplated the rapid growth of ride-sharing services, advances in autonomous vehicle technology, mounting global environmental concerns, and the megatrend of increasing urbanization, they realized the jobs to be done people rely on their personal cars to solve would fragment. Simply getting from point A to point B could be accomplished with increasing ease and at lower cost through ride-sharing services. Same for the occasional need to haul large items—just order an UberXL. Meanwhile, congested cities increasingly prioritize alternate forms of transportation— and all this would happen before the disruptions that fully autonomous vehicles will likely cause. If the auto executives didn't redefine their company around an expanded concept of mobility it might become obsolete.

Developing these sorts of insights requires you to enter the learning mode we discussed in chapter 2 and diverge for a bit to explore trends and then, through debate and discussion, converge on a core set of assumptions about the future. This demands a highly intuitive approach, and intuition is fed by a diversity of inputs. You should prepare for these strategic dialogues well before they begin—reading extensively, having wide-ranging conversations with colleagues, making time to reflect on your emerging assumptions, and visiting start-ups, cutting-edge laboratories, and businesses in frontier markets.

Executives almost always push to get on with it at this point— to hurry up and get to the business decisions they need to make. It's critical that you remain patient for two reasons. First, you don't want your view of the future to be influenced by your business's current priorities, which will inevitably distort it. Failing to spend the time you need to diligently probe the future environment makes it easier to fall back into present-forward thinking. Second, the picture of the future that you develop will have to feel as real to you as anything else in your purview.

If you and your team are going to believe in your future state vision on a gut level—and you will have to if you are going to be able to convince others to feel the same way—you will need to take the time to really soak in it and reflect on its implications together. This can't be rushed.

View of the World Statements

One effective tool for consolidating all your inputs into a distinct point of view that your whole team can align on is to develop a set of view of the world statements. These articulate specific assumptions about how things will work in the future environment in a way that is precise and quantifiable when possible, and that will ultimately shape your strategic response. For example, an automotive company might focus on rapid increases in the production and sales of electric vehicles. A corresponding view of the world statement might be something like, "By 2030, 50 percent of all new cars sold globally will be electric."

We often develop these statements by collecting twenty or thirty key assumptions about what the future might hold. Then we survey a broad group of executives, asking them to rate each assumption on its likelihood and impact. As themes emerge from their responses, we pressure test the outliers—things that are assumed to be unlikely but might reflect organizational blind spots. After the list has been culled and synthesized, we bring it into a strategic dialogue, where the leadership team can debate it further, ultimately landing on a handful of factors that represent a consensus view. The act of pinning down these assumptions—and even more importantly, of going through the exercise as a team—forces them to focus on their strategic implications.

Automotive View of the World Statements 2030
Key assumptions related to major driving forces of change in the automotive industry

---

AUTONOMY

The adoption of semi-autonomous vehicles is common across vehicle segments and is not a differentiator for OEMs.

Fully autonomous vehicles will be significantly intertwined with electric vehicle solutions and will comprise 10% of the market, leading to fundamental shifts in personal and fleet-based mobility systems.

As the autonomous vehicles (AV) industry grows, customers will demand to be more productive and more entertained within their mobility experiences.

ELECTRIFICATION

Government mandates may require OEMs to use specific technologies (e.g., battery electric vehicles, fuel cell vehicles) to sell in key markets such as North America and China, and/or major cities globally.

Excluding regulatory incentives, cost of ownership for electric vehicles is on par with internal combustion vehicles in the 2030-2035 timeframe, depending on regional conditions and technology advancement.

Charging infrastructure is widely available in key markets (e.g., North America, Europe, and China).

CITIES

Telematics enables broader connectivity of vehicles and data-driven services (e.g., logistics management, insurance, real-time maps), creating new business models starting in commercial fleets.

Sharing (e.g., taxi, AVs) is the primary mode of transportation for many consumers in high-density urban areas.

Cities become aggregators of mobility demand and arbiters of solution providers.

Remember, the goal is not to predict the future with certainty (nobody can) but to paint an impressionist painting of it detailed enough to build clarity and alignment on what will have to be done to meet its challenges and opportunities. To this end, we often design meeting formats different in tone and approach than the typical PowerPoint-driven strategic review. Unconventional meeting formats risk coming off as contrived if not facilitated well, but they can powerfully engage and align a group of leaders when managed effectively.

An example of this is a meeting a group of our colleagues led with the vice chancellor, deputy vice chancellors, school deans, and functional leaders of Australia's Deakin University.

The meeting was called to assess the future of higher education and the university's readiness for it. The executives gathered in a room hung with five visually engaging posters. Each poster focused on a macro theme, such as what, where, and how students will study in the future and the resulting key strategic questions each posed. We developed the posters through our own research, interviews with each member of the leadership team, and a survey of the university's top three hundred leaders. Participants started the meeting sitting around a big U-shaped table with the presenter in the middle but then quickly did something different: they got up and moved around, with small groups forming around each poster. We gave them time to absorb and discuss the material, rotating the groups from poster to poster every ten minutes. After that, we split the group into two: one half of the room was designated "optimists" and charged with making the case for a bright future in which Deakin is ready to embrace the changes implied by the posters. The other half were "pessimists," charged with making the case for why change would be difficult and even unmanageable. They prepared their arguments and then had a spirited debate across the room.

"The end is not near—it's here," argued one group. "We have evolved in the past, and we'll evolve again," countered the other. As the teams went back and forth, exploring different facets of the future and what it meant for them, a resolve to embrace the future became apparent.

After a short break we asked the participants to locate themselves, physically, along a spectrum we had laid out on the floor, with the most optimistic at one end and the most pessimistic at the other. Then, we called on each of them to explain why they were standing where they were. By the end of the meeting, all of the leaders, self-described pessimists and optimists alike, agreed to seize a set of future-oriented opportunities.

Step 2: Identify the Major Implications of the Future for Your Enterprise

Now that you have a sense of the mechanics of the world you'll be designing for, it's time to put your company into it. You've asserted what your markets will be like; next you have to figure out what that means for you. To do that, imagine how your current businesses will fare in that envisioned future. Will they still have a role to play? What will have to be true for them to thrive? What does that mean for your growth prospects?

At this stage leaders often realize that business-as-usual has a greater downside risk than they'd supposed and that there will be unrealized upside, as new opportunities will arise that are beyond the scope of their current businesses. Projecting the current status and health of your core business into the future allows you to define your growth gap—the difference between what you aspire to (or are expected to) deliver and what you are likely to. The relative size of the gap bounds the relative size of the response you'll have to muster, as we will discuss further in chapter 4.

The major implications for your business generally fall within one of the four archetypes that we describe below. Note that we call these *archetypes* rather than *scenarios* because scenarios, in the classic sense of scenario planning, are different views of what an uncertain industry future might turn out to be. They generally present a variety of best and worst cases that are extrapolated from your present circumstances; their purpose is to help you prepare to respond to one contingency or another. Developing multiple scenarios does not provide the North Star that a single powerful vision can.

Our implication archetypes, in contrast, describe what the future is likely to *mean*, based on a tactile, multidimensional understanding of the major changes likely to occur in your markets and your customers' needs. The mental processes you and your team use to develop and align on these assumptions may overlap with some you would use in scenario planning, but the aim is not to cover all your bases but, as much as possible, to develop a perspective on what will truly matter so you can respond to it in the right way.

Sometimes leadership teams know immediately which archetype best describes their outlook, but usually it is difficult for them to converge on one. Once again, no one has a crystal ball; there is no data that can tell us with certainty how things will actually play out. We often lead our clients through an exploratory assessment, relying on judgment and nuance, and requiring time for debate and reflection. Together, we think through questions such as, *At a high level, across the totality of your businesses and markets, under which rubric do you fall? Are you facing a revolution or an evolution?* Then we prompt them to take a more granular look: *Which archetype best describes each of your key product lines? Are there geographic differences? What would have to be true for your key business units to be described by one implications archetype or another?*

Then we ask our clients to pull back and consider things from the outside in. *What will your customers have to say about your offerings in the future state? Will they remain loyal, or will they look*

Four Archetypal Implications for Your Future

Major Threats on the Horizon

Significant disruption is on the horizon, posing **a mortal threat** to current businesses and calling for a **thoroughly transformative strategy**, both a major repositioning of the core business and the development of new growth businesses. Think of Kodak as digital imaging technology emerged, or Blockbuster Video stores after Netflix introduced its subscribe-through-the-mail business model.

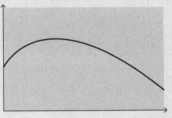

Disrupted core business leads to decline

Moderate Threats Emerge

The growth prospects in your core businesses are hitting their limits as they mature; disruption or commoditization is coming, but it **won't necessarily be fatal**, at least for the foreseeable future. Think of the challenges facing consumer product companies that sell branded staples, like shampoos and skin-care products, in the face of competition enabled by e-commerce platforms. **Current businesses will need to be transformed** with new business models and/or augmented by new growth platforms.

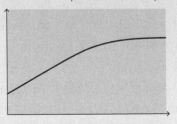

Disrupted core business slows growth

Major Opportunities Ahead

Your current businesses are reasonably positioned for sustained growth with some targeted adjustments, but they **will not realize major growth opportunities unless they develop the new platforms** that can and should be built alongside them. Think of Amazon and its seemingly 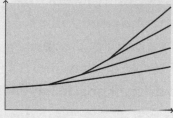 limitless expansion in e-commerce, alongside its development of adjacent businesses in cloud computing, logistics, and the like.

Add growth platforms
to the core

Maintain the Status Quo

Doubling down and focusing on business-as-usual is the right choice. For this to be true (and to be frank, it rarely is, given the accelerating pace of change—just look what's happening to traditional grocery stores, an industry that was relatively stable for decades, now that Amazon has moved into the space and online delivery services are on the rise), you'd have to believe that **you have significant headroom for growth** or that **you lack** 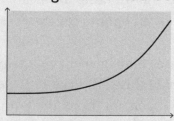 **the ability to pursue new growth opportunities**. We include this option cautiously because it will be tempting for many executives to default to it, whether it applies to their cases or not.

Focus on growth
in the core

elsewhere for new sources of value? In order to comfortably place yourself in Major Opportunities or Maintain the Status Quo, you would have to believe that your current model will still deliver unsurpassed value to your customers. That should be a real gut check.

> The aha moment that comes out of this work isn't always a brilliant new thought or a penetrating analysis. Often it comes from a place of emotion, as leaders let go of their defensive denials and embrace a reality that they had subconsciously anticipated or feared.

We often see this happen with businesses on a path to commoditization that aren't yet in crisis. Growth is more difficult to come by, competitors are moving faster than before, customers are less loyal. The platform isn't burning, but it's smoldering, and if you're paying attention you can smell the smoke. And yet, one way or another, you've managed to pull a rabbit out of a hat and hit your profitability numbers, quarter after quarter. Maybe you believe you can keep on doing that indefinitely—"We've figured it out before, we'll figure it out again." Confronting the future head on, when procrastination is no longer an option, can have a salutary unsticking effect.

The executive team at the diabetes management company we mentioned earlier had an epiphany of this sort. Prior to the exercise, commoditization had never been far from their minds, though it was never squarely in focus. Once they acknowledged the threat, their anxiety turned to excitement as they realized that the same forces leading to commoditization could open up much bigger opportunities for them, much as the commoditization of the PC had led Apple to develop its digital hub strategy. As products in the diabetes company's space became increasingly software-oriented and digitally enabled, value would shift from hardware (blood glucose meters) to services (personalized diabetes management solutions). Freed from the need to think solely within the boundaries of their existing product lines, they began to pursue those new possibilities.

We've seen this dynamic play out with a wide range of other clients, from a professional services firm that came to terms with the likelihood that its people-focused model would be increasingly disrupted by AI-fueled digital services, to a medical device company that began to shift its customer focus from product performance-oriented surgeons to bottom line-oriented hospital executives.

William Hait's team had its aha moment at an offsite, where senior leaders absorbed case studies of disruption in other industries and drew connections to their own experiences. They didn't expect the world to change overnight or for the pharmaceutical business as they knew it to be eclipsed (Major Threats). At the same time, they couldn't imagine a world in which Janssen wasn't playing a key role in the emerging new paradigm (Maintain Status Quo). On a case-by-case basis, they believed their circumstances fell under either Moderate Threats or Major Opportunities. The new disease interception paradigm, they realized, would manifest at different rates for different disease areas. The old paradigm might persist for decades for conditions in which scientific understanding was less mature, whereas the new one was already present in areas like cholesterol management.

Ultimately, they agreed they weren't talking about displacing their current business with a new model but rather augmenting it with a set of future-facing growth platforms (Major Opportunities). Janssen's highly successful core business would continue to innovate on its current trajectory, while new efforts that accelerated the development of what they came to call a World Without Disease would be launched alongside it, focused on innovative drugs but also on whatever else it would take to realize the vision—be it consumer health products, medical devices, or digital therapeutics. This allowed them to leverage J&J's unique assets and capabilities across all of its sectors as well as its open innovation ecosystem, which features a leading venture capital arm and a network of innovation centers and start-up incubators around the world.

Step 3: Envision the Future State of Your Business

Having developed a point of view on the future and come to terms with its implications for your existing businesses, it's time to focus on what you will offer as part of your envisioned future state, how you will create value, and how you'll address your looming growth, positioning, and capability gaps in doing so. We find it helpful to systematically think through three tried and true growth categories:

- **Core:** Opportunities to extend or evolve your core offerings to maximize their relevance in the future environment.

- **Adjacencies:** Distinct new products and services that can augment your core offerings or opportunities to take your core offerings into different geographies and markets, with either option (or combined options) leveraging the existing business model.

- **New growth:** Growth initiatives that may leverage core capabilities of the organization but in new and distinct businesses, typically with new business models.

Comprehensive future-back strategies leverage all three. Apple continued to make computers (its core business), but it also developed new software like iTunes, iPhoto, iMovie, and so on to enable its digital hub strategy (an adjacency). Finally, it began to create new products in new categories to fully realize the strategy—the iPod, the iPhone, and the iPad—that also unlocked new business models, like profiting off of media and app sales on their platforms.

The need to focus on both core and new categories is obvious to most of our clients. Less obvious, but always critical, are adjacencies. When done right, adjacencies offer near-term revenue while building bridges to the future. For example, a pharmacy chain we worked with asserted a vision in which it excelled at delivering healthcare to its customers, powered by a range of new technology-enabled capabilities. But a first, low-tech step—an adjacent move—was to reframe the role of the pharmacist. After receiving targeted training on key drivers of outcomes like medication adherence and care management after discharge from the hospital, pharmacists were moved out from behind their counters to meet with customers in more consultative settings. This simple move yielded immediate value while opening up further possibilities for healthcare delivery down the road.

As with the exercises described earlier, the visions you develop for your core, adjacent, and new growth businesses will be richer if you engage in multiple rounds of debate and discussion, supported by targeted analyses. Put ideas down on paper, tease them out with colleagues and outside experts, and refine them. Start by asserting—at a high-level, in snapshots—who your customers will be, the main product lines you'll offer them, the geographies you'll cover, and the business models you'll leverage. Ground your ideas in analysis, but don't rely too heavily on data, as no data set will be accurate enough to drive your decisions.

Aspirations and Purpose

Use your deepest aspirations as your touchstone. A medical technology manufacturer we worked with was struggling to commit to developing robotics platforms. They saw their potential, but they also recognized that they would necessitate difficult and expensive changes to their sales and service model. What finally got them over the hump was an appeal to their sense of purpose. They'd always been a leader in surgical technology; this was core to their identity. Could they still think of themselves as leaders if they passed up this opportunity? Going back to their sense of purpose gave them the fortitude to make the leap.

The executive team at Ascension, one of the leading nonprofit health systems in the United States, had a similar epiphany when going through a future-back process to define their strategic direction for the next decade. As a Catholic institution, Ascension is deeply mission-driven, focused on delivering spiritually centered, holistic care to the communities it serves. Early in the process, they undertook jobs to be done research to make sure they were in touch with evolving consumer expectations, and they were confronted by a difficult reality: most consumers did not define their health in terms of hospital care or many of the other services Ascension offered. Rather, they defined their health in terms of their broader life goals and their day-to-day needs. In fact, many regarded their ability to stay out of the healthcare system altogether as a measure of their long-term health. For Ascension to become truly central to the health of its communities, it had to become much more than a hospital system.

So they developed a transformational vision for the future of healthcare and their role in it, one that addressed consumers' wellness needs in a variety of physical and virtual settings. "Fundamental to this shift," Ascension's former CEO Anthony Tersigni wrote in *The Journal of Healthcare Management*, "is reimagining all aspects of care from the point of view of consumers rather than addressing their needs based on traditional volume-based, hospital-centric models."[2]

In many ways, this was a return to the spirit of the religious women and men who founded the original hospitals that became Ascension Health, and better fulfilled its stated mission of serving "all persons, especially those living in poverty and who are struggling the most."[3]

To do this yourself, ask what your company could be in its envisioned future. *What role could and should it play? What would best serve its legacy and values? What would be deeply meaningful and inspiring to your employees and other stakeholders?* Once again, don't let your current structure—your product lines, the markets you're in, how you're organized—get in the way. This is your opportunity to design the ideal company of the future, irrespective—for now—of what it is today. This is the essence of future-back thinking.

While innovative drugs would still play a prominent role in Janssen's envisioned future, they would also develop adjacent and new solution areas—novel ways to screen for and identify people on the path to disease, better ways to measure and monitor them to determine the right moment of intervention, and digital and consumer-oriented health products for people who, in many cases, are not yet patients and therefore face different cost/benefit and risk/benefit tradeoffs than people who are already sick. Just as crucial were the new business models that would allow both patients and nonpatients to take advantage of those solutions by ensuring their affordability.

Strategic Narrative

At this point, your vision should take a narrative form: you should be able to tell a succinct story about what the future will hold, what it means for you, and how your company will shape it. It should be exciting, galvanizing, and imbued with purpose, so it will inspire your internal and external stakeholders, breaking down at least some of the barriers to long-term thinking described earlier in this book.

So many executives complain that they have no choice but to stick to their knitting, lest Wall Street, with its short-term expectations, punish them for trying to do something new. We've worked with many Wall Street analysts, and all of them have addressed this issue in more or less these words: "Tell your clients to explain the what and the why of their vision and where they're trying to take their companies. If they treat us like mushrooms and keep us in the dark, of course we're going to be skeptical." To get Wall Street on your side, you need to tell them a hopeful story.

Here is what the Janssen team wrote:

Janssen's Vision of a World without Disease

We envision a world in which widespread disease is a historical artifact; where all people live healthier lives promoted by technological and medical advances; and where life science companies discover and deploy solutions that effectively prevent, intercept and cure disease. In line with our commitment to transformational medical innovation and our mission to change the trajectory of health for humanity, we will accelerate the development of healthcare solutions that eliminate disease.

We will develop comprehensive strategies in disease areas most ready for the new paradigm, identifying people at risk of developing disease, monitoring disease-causing processes, and intervening with clinically proven therapies to intercept the development of disease. We will work closely with partners across Johnson & Johnson to develop world-class healthcare products, and with partners in the broader biomedical research ecosystem to develop the technologies, solutions, regulatory protocols and business models that will accelerate the realization of our vision.[4]

Compare that with a typical corporate vision statement: "We will be the number one preferred supplier of health products and services, dominating in the markets we choose to serve and recognized as the top place to work." Which company would you prefer to devote your energy, creativity, and time to?

Having developed your vision, now it is time to translate it into a strategy, which is the subject of chapter 4.

Chapter 4

CONVERTING VISION TO STRATEGY

Planning is bringing the future
into the present so that you
can do something about it now.

—Alan Lakein

From storyteller to engineer • The three portfolios: future state, innovation, and investment • Bridging the growth gap: strategic opportunity areas • Walking the strategy back • What to slow down / what to shut down • The three portfolios as a system • You can't reap what you don't sow • When to "burn the boats"

When a leading defense contractor reviewed its long-term strategy in 2010, they projected current industry trends and business prospects out to 2020. The results were reassuring: its pipeline of new and existing contracts would sustain revenue growth at exactly the rate they wanted (which was to exceed GDP year over year).

Two years later, when they engaged us to help them with long-term innovation, we suggested they take a less present-forward approach to their future. Set your planning horizon all the way out to 2030, we said, a date well past the lifetimes of a number of their existing contracts. This time, the results were troubling. While they did surface some promising opportunities, they realized they couldn't bank on continuing results from all of their existing programs, since many had little to no likelihood of being renewed. While they went into the exercise thinking they fit into the Major Opportunities archetype we described in the previous chapter, it became clear their businesses were facing Moderate and Major Threats.

"What got us here will not get us to the future," the CEO glumly concluded.

In the series of executive dialogues that followed, we worked with the CEO and his senior team to envision possible US civil agency applications that could help to fill the gap, as well as a set of new and different businesses in commercial markets they could develop for the different ecosystem they would be competing in. Instead of tailoring their growth aspirations to the vicissitudes of military budgets and Pentagon procurement cycles as they unfolded from the present forward, they could change the competitive landscape from the future back by proactively developing a set of products their potential customers didn't yet know they would need.

Their work had only just begun. Having a well-developed vision is crucial, but it is never enough; you also need a concrete plan to make that vision real. This calls for a shift in mindset, from storyteller to engineer, that is accomplished by delineating and systemizing a set of business choices. In this chapter, we will take you through the process by which a vision is converted to a long-term strategy. Then that strategy is walked back to the present, in the form of a set of prioritized and funded growth initiatives. Each must have clearly demarcated starting points, explicitly denoted investments, and specific milestones to measure its progress.

The Three Portfolios

We have found that the best way to convert a vision to strategic choices linking the future to the present is to think in terms of filling and balancing a set of three linked and interdependent portfolios. The future state portfolio is typically a financial projection of your enterprise at your target end date, in which your high-level assertions about your future businesses are translated into dollars and cents. The innovation portfolio is a set of planned

Phase II: Convert Vision to Strategy

Step 1: Develop the future state portfolio

- Quantify your growth gap
- Strategic opportunity areas (SOAs)

Step 2: Walk the future back

- Develop milestones

Step 3: The innovation & investment portfolios

- Categorize initiatives
- Balance by growth, risk, and return
- Decide what to stop, start, and continue

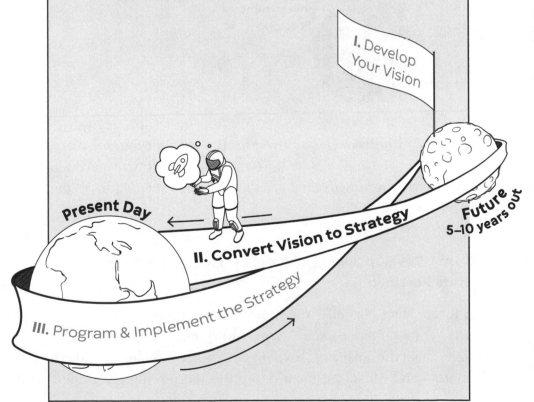

Vision Is Converted to Strategy via the Development of Three Interdependent Portfolios

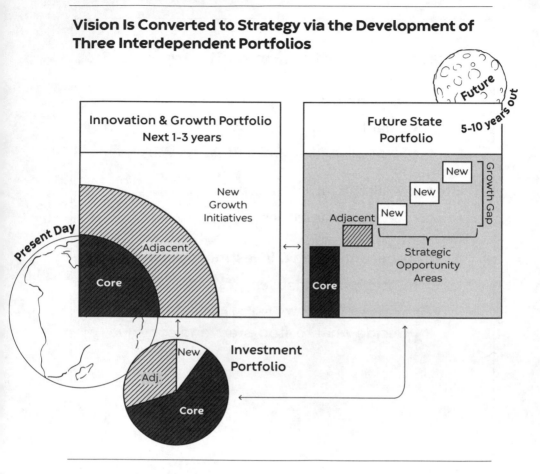

projects or initiatives, prioritized for the next one to three years, that reflect the future state portfolio. The investment portfolio specifies the resources (in dollars and people) that will fund the innovation portfolio.

Step 1: Develop Your Long-Term Strategy—The Future State Portfolio

A future state portfolio is a visual representation of your enterprise at its target end state. Here, you've made high-level assertions about the business—covering core, adjacent, and new growth efforts—and translated them into projected revenues or profits.

Since long-term value is driven by top-line growth, we generally encourage clients to think in terms of revenues rather than profits; however, there are exceptions. For institutions in the nonprofit or government sectors, we recommend that you substitute projections of relative importance or magnitude. For example, a research institution could delineate the number of major programs it would run per research area. The impact of a public health initiative can be measured by the number of lives it touches. Regardless of whether you benchmark revenues, profits, or impact, the act of projecting out each effort and weighing its status as part of a portfolio makes your vision more tangible.

Future State Portfolio

The growth gap is determined by the difference between your growth aspiration and what your core and adjacent businesses can deliver in the future

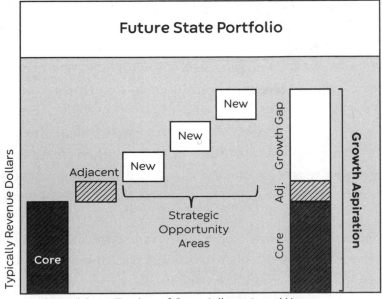

Like picking the right time horizon, setting a topline growth aspiration merits considerable debate and discussion. Sometimes companies already have a clear goal they can simply extend into the future, such as wanting to exceed GDP year over year (as the defense contractor did) or sustaining a commitment to shareholders of delivering 5 percent annual revenue growth. Other times they rally around a simple and memorable aim, like doubling the business in a decade. Spend the time you need to develop a target that is both aspirational and realistic and that the full team can get behind. Then debate and develop explicit assumptions about how much growth each of your core and adjacent businesses can deliver. Put simply, the larger the difference between your aspiration and what your core and adjacencies can deliver (your growth gap), the more you'll have to stretch beyond them.

Knowing when your growth gap will develop helps you determine the pace and scale of the new business activities you'll need to fill it. For example, if you have a moderately sized gap (say, 10 to 20 percent of revenues seven years out) but expect it to grow gradually, you likely have time to develop new businesses organically. If, however, you anticipate your gap emerging sooner, you'll need to be more aggressive and consider buying your way into new businesses. Most companies we work with land on a hybrid approach, with mergers and acquisitions in some lines of business and organic development in others.

Once you've quantified your growth gap, we generally recommend that you divide it by three or four and then create three or four major areas of beyond-the-core growth, or what we call strategic opportunity areas (SOAs), that can fill it. That makes sense as a starting point, because it's too risky to place bets on just one or two SOAs, given the likelihood that they won't all pan out. On the other hand, most organizations have trouble funding and managing five or more at the same time.

When you've determined how big each line of business must be to fill your gap by your target date, use abductive reasoning (as

Strategic Opportunity Areas (SOAs)

Think of SOAs as fishing holes, each representing a market in which you can play and win, and where every fish is a potential business idea that can provide the beyond-the-core growth you need. SOAs should be broad enough to include a range of possibilities, but specific enough that they can frame one or more initiatives that you can begin today.

WHAT
Important, unsatisfied, and widely held customer jobs to be done

WHO
Target market or customer

SOA

HOW
Potential technologies and solutions leveraging key company capabilities

WHY
Future trends and implications

discussed in chapter 2) to pressure test how well your future state portfolio hangs together. Ask questions like: *What would we have to believe for a business in market x to attain $y million of net new*

Defense Contractor Future State Portfolio 15 Years Out

The company envisioned a set of core and beyond-the-core businesses to address their projected **revenue** growth gap*

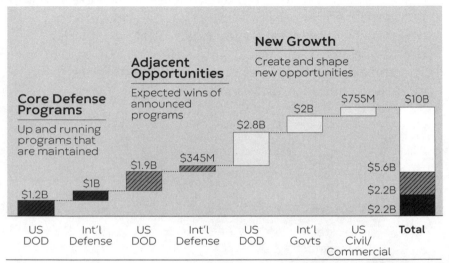

*All figures, descriptions and proportions are disguised

growth by year z? Can we assume the overall market will grow fast enough to make that a realistic proposition? Analyses like these can give you more reason to believe your strategic picture is in the right ballpark, or it can warn you that it's not—in which case you'll need to revise your vision. The defense contractor's future state portfolio is shown above.

An industrials company we worked with had originally thought they fit into implication archetype 3 (Major Opportunities), so they focused most of their thinking on profitability while placing a few bets on early-stage but high-potential areas beyond their core (plastics and climate solutions). But as they began to develop their future state portfolio, they realized that one of their higher-risk business divisions no longer fit their strategy. If they divested it, they could not achieve the net growth they needed. This meant that, like the defense contractor, they actually fit into implication archetype 2 (Moderate Threats). Commoditization was more imminent than they'd previously understood; the beyond-the-core

Industrials Company Future State Portfolio 5 Years Out

The company envisioned a set of core and beyond-the-core businesses to address their projected **profit** growth gap*

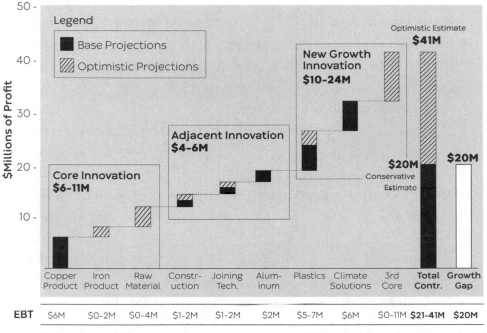

| EBT | $6M | $0-2M | $0-4M | $1-2M | $1-2M | $2M | $5-7M | $6M | $0-11M | $21-41M | $20M |

Earnings before taxes (EBT)   *All figures, descriptions, and proportions are disguised.

growth they thought they might pursue as an option was in fact quite necessary. So they decided to accelerate those early bets while undertaking a high-potential M&A opportunity as well. As shown in the chart above, they pegged the potential of those three initiatives in profits due to their need to lock down their near-term profitability forecasts.

Step 2: Walk the Future Back—Milestones Development

Once you have defined your future state portfolio, the next step is to walk it back to the present. To do this, you work backwards from your future state, setting milestones at roughly two- to three-year intervals. Now you are moving from SOAs to the actual business initiatives you can develop to exploit them. If you've set your future state portfolio at a distance of ten years, first you'll define what has to be true in eight years to take the next step to year ten. Ask yourself: *What will your portfolio mix across core and new businesses be? What new capabilities and business structures will need to be in place? How mature will each of your new initiatives be?* Next, you'll move to year six and so on, moving back two to three years at a time and setting explicit benchmarks for each stage until you land in the present.

It can be overwhelming to contemplate the implications of visionary strategies. Setting achievable near-term goals for your efforts (for example, key talent hired, programs launched, proof of concept achieved, partnerships developed, M&A deals executed) instills confidence, creates momentum, and ensures accountability.

Transformational strategies can take a long time to show significant results; the curve often looks more like a hockey stick than a diagonal line. The walk back should account for this, allowing

---

Milestone Development the Future-back Way
Walk back from your desired future state, setting milestones at roughly 2- to 3-year intervals.

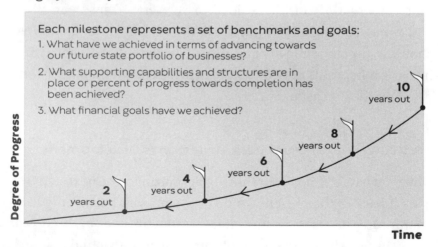

Each milestone represents a set of benchmarks and goals:
1. What have we achieved in terms of advancing towards our future state portfolio of businesses?
2. What supporting capabilities and structures are in place or percent of progress towards completion has been achieved?
3. What financial goals have we achieved?

Degree of Progress

2 years out
4 years out
6 years out
8 years out
10 years out

Time

sufficient time for initiatives to incubate or explicitly defining the parameters for M&A to more quickly plug gaps. The importance of setting these milestones from the future back—starting with the end state and working backwards to the present—cannot be overstated. If a strategy is simply extrapolated from the present forward, your existing processes, rules, norms, and metrics will get in your way. Developing it from the future back reduces the likelihood that you will perpetuate your existing realities.

Step 3: Develop the Innovation and Investment Portfolios

The walk back lands in the innovation portfolio, which includes all of the core, adjacent, and new growth initiatives intended to deliver the growth defined in the future state portfolio, as well as any capability-building initiatives required. Striking the right balance between core and new growth efforts is extraordinarily challenging, as there are deep management challenges associated with allocating for the future while also managing for today. This was the subject of the recent book *Dual Transformation: How to Reposition Today's Business While Creating the Future* that Mark cowrote with our Innosight colleagues Scott Anthony and Clark Gilbert, which is in many ways a companion to this one.[1] We will return to the principles it laid out in chapter 5, which covers programming and implementation.

We set the horizon for the innovation portfolio at one to three years, so that it covers both ongoing initiatives and placeholders for new ones, as well as any M&A efforts that will have to be chartered. To do this on your own, simply sort your programs into buckets covering core, adjacent, and new. Each should have distinct expectations for growth, risk, and return. Core projects are your bread and butter; they come with limited upsides but high degrees of certainty. You know how to execute tweaks and more significant changes to them as needed. New growth projects, on

Linking Future Opportunities with Today's Initiatives

The envisioned Strategic Opportunity Areas (SOAs) and adjacencies in the Future State portfolio are walked back to the present in the form of the planned initiatives in the Innovation and Growth Portfolio. The Investment Portfolio allocates dollars between core, adjacent, and new growth initiatives.

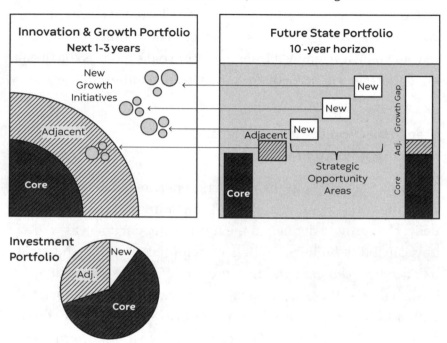

the other hand, are options for the future—they come with significant uncertainty but lots of potential.

At the same time, you need to develop an investment portfolio, in which you formalize your decisions about where to invest and where your resources will come from. In building it, you should measure dollars but also people and leadership mindshare, as talent and leadership energy are often more scarce in big companies than seed funding. Set ideal targets for proportional spending across core, adjacent, and new initiatives, and measure how far off you are. This frames your most difficult choices, as you'll likely need to cut funding or slow down or stop initiatives in some places to pay for increases in others. This is where you make further calls on which programs won't fit into

Growth, Risk, and Return Expectations

Think of your innovation and investment portfolios as you might a personal portfolio of investments, balancing growth, risk, and return across "asset classes"

	Growth Potential	Risk	Return
Core	Low to Medium	Low	**Optimize:** provides steady base but not sufficient to ensure returns; optimize to free up cash flow for other investments
Adjacent	Medium to High	Medium	**Maximize:** best near-term opportunities to augment growth; be prepared to invest aggressively when warranted
New	High	High	**Protect:** highly uncertain but highest potential; place targeted bets and have the patience to let them develop over time

your overall future state. Given that all of your programs have vested interests and influential sponsors, it is likely to be extremely difficult to slow down or stop any of them. Looking into the future, defining a future state portfolio, and then walking it back to the present via the innovation and investment portfolio provides perspective that makes the need for those kinds of decisions much clearer.

Future-back strategy is always about the allocation (and reallocation) of scarce resources. Any new strategy will cost money and require the dedication of top talent. Having a clearly articulated vision is highly clarifying as there will always be programs that can be deprioritized, reshaped, or divested.

> **One of the most critical aspects of the three portfolios work is deciding what to slow down or shut down.**

A. G. Lafley told us that when he began his second stint as Procter & Gamble's CEO, he made a strategic decision to weed the garden, selling off businesses in at least half a dozen of P&G's industry categories, including fragrances, hair coloring, food and beverage, and cooking oil. All of the brands in those categories were profitable, he said, but they were prone to commoditization. As he put it, "Our strategy, in Peter Drucker's terms, was one of systematic abandonment. We wanted to free up the scarce resources, people, and cash to fund the innovations that were necessary to enter new businesses and transform important existing businesses."[2]

How the Three Portfolios Work Together

The three portfolios are interdependent and dynamic. They are interdependent because their three views must always hang together. If you are projecting a future state portfolio featuring 30 percent net new growth, then the project mix in your innovation portfolio must be set up to deliver it, and the resource allocations in your investment portfolio must be sufficient to fund the projects. They are dynamic because these views are highly iterative; the model must be continually updated and tracked as you reshape your vision based on the new learning that comes over time.

It's also key to understand that you can't reap what you don't sow; your resource limitations will constrain how ambitious your future state and innovation portfolios can be. If you find it hard to fund new initiatives simply by turning off old ones, then you'll need a more fundamental transformation of your cost base to ensure sustainable cash flows. Needless to say, contemplating and committing to major transformations are moments of truth in which executive teams must look each other in the eye and agree to "burn the boats," just as Cortez did when he landed with his men at Veracruz. There can be no turning back.

Dr. Hait and his team didn't need to burn any boats—Janssen's core business had plenty of upside. But they did have to make their vision real. Johnson & Johnson had annual revenues of about $76 billion. Its diversified portfolio included twenty-seven brands or platforms (twelve in pharmaceuticals, twelve in medical devices, three in consumer health) that generated at least $1 billion in annual revenues. Any new growth platforms had to achieve that kind of scale to be relevant. So they carved out a start-up budget for their new initiatives by pruning their portfolio of innovation programs that were no longer on-strategy, and they prepared to launch a series of new projects to build toward their vision.

Armed with your three portfolios, you now have a strategy connecting your vision for the future of your markets to a concrete plan for what you must do today to bring it to life. But just as a vision requires a strategy, a strategy must be carefully programmed before it can be implemented, which is a multifaceted challenge calling for a multifaceted approach. In chapter 5, we'll take you through phase 3 of the future-back process.

Chapter 5

PROGRAMMING AND IMPLEMENTING YOUR STRATEGY

The right strategy is never more than 49 percent of the problem.

—Joseph Bower

A new strategy must first be programmed • Future-oriented activities and the role of the senior team • Minimally viable bureaucracy • The master plan • Breakthrough innovation teams • Incubator designs • A discovery-driven approach • Implementation—incubating, accelerating, and transitioning • There is always more future ahead of us

---

A few years ago, we worked through our future-back process with the leadership team of a midsized manufacturing company. The future state portfolio we developed together was focused on achieving much greater profitability than its commoditizing core businesses could deliver, and the strategic path we laid out to achieve its aims was clearly defined. But when we suggested to our client that it was time to step back and carefully consider how each of their new initiatives should be governed, organized, funded, and implemented, they demurred.

"Execution is what we do," they argued. "We know how to manage the work."

A year later, we got a call from the CEO, who was frustrated that the strategy hadn't gained enough traction; progress was much harder and slower than he'd ever imagined. We reminded him that while execution within the core business might be an area of consummate strength for his firm, the implementation of a transformative, long-term strategy requires a different set of processes and overall capabilities.

Phase III: Program and Implement Your Visionary Strategy

Step 1: Programming

The Role of the Senior Leadership Team
- Governance
- Transformation management office
- Master plan and funding

Organizational Model for Innovation Teams
- Teams and talent
- Incubator designs

Setting Up the Right Process
- Explore, envision, and discover

Step 2: Implementation

Three Stages of New Growth Initiatives
- Incubation
- Acceleration
- Transition

Setting Anchors

I. Develop Your Vision

Present Day

II. Convert Vision to Strategy

Future 5–10 years out

III. Program & Implement the Strategy

Their situation was not unique. A survey of nearly two thousand executives conducted in 2015 found that only 26 percent had faith that their company's transformative strategies would succeed.[1] Much of their pessimism, no doubt, can be ascribed to their companies' past failures to develop a compelling vision and commit to the right strategies to achieve it. But just as significant is the fact that most organizations leap reflexively from strategy to execution, using the structures, processes, rules, and norms that guide the execution of their core businesses to carry out their outside-the-core initiatives, which inevitably constrains or distorts their intended outcomes.

> Just as a vision needs to be translated into a strategy, a strategy must be carefully programmed into an organization before it can be effectively implemented.

That is what William Hait did with the World Without Disease initiative. First, he recruited Ben Wiegand, a Johnson & Johnson R&D executive with extensive experience managing innovation, to build and lead a new group to pursue its portfolio of projects. Then they set up a small, purpose-built organization designed to move fast in an uncertain, risky environment, with a streamlined governance model that allowed for rapid decision making.

They focused on a set of disease areas that were the ripest for the new paradigm and that had the most realistic chances of becoming medically and financially significant in a relevant timeframe. One of them was lung cancer. Years of exposure to carcinogens from smoking or environmental pollution damages the lungs, leading to premalignancies that can theoretically be treated if they are detected in time. A second targeted colorectal cancer, as discussed in chapter 3. The third addressed type-1 diabetes, an autoimmune disease that most often strikes young children, disabling the insulin-producing beta cells in the pancreas, forcing a lifetime of dependence on insulin injections. Emerging research has identified an escalating series of indicators, traceable in blood samples, that signal when a child is on the path to developing insulin dependence, opening windows for early interception.

Keeping their future state goals closely in mind, Wiegand's group launched a slate of ventures. Each was led by an expert in the targeted disease area and tapped into broad networks of support. Each would be funded through its next milestone and then either shut down or escalated depending on its results. The idea was to strike fast (relatively, that is—biopharma development timelines are typically ten-plus years) in order to prove out the model. Some of these projects leveraged existing assets that could be accelerated; others focused on external investments and partnerships that were already making progress and could be brought in-house if their efforts succeeded. In an interview, Wiegand noted:

> The key for us was to break our highly aspirational vision down into achievable milestones that we could easily communicate. We walked the vision back from ten years out to the handful of things we needed to accomplish by the end of the year to know we're moving in the right direction at the right pace—always showing management how our initial milestones ladder up to the vision.
>
> In the first year it was all about picking our top few focus areas, hiring world class leaders in each, and launching what we call "killer experiments." We could get management aligned to these, and then demonstrate our success in a very real and tangible way.[2]

Achieving results, scaling programs that were working, and quickly shutting down programs that weren't increased management's belief in the team, unlocking additional support.

Step 1: Programming Your Strategy

Intentional approaches to setting up and managing a portfolio of new growth activities are essential for almost every visionary strategy. Corporations allocate resources, govern lines of business, and manage performance through management systems. Point solutions will inevitably get swallowed up by the existing system, which is already deeply entrenched. Systems-level challenges demand systems-level responses.

When programming a breakthrough strategy, you must design and assemble a set of components that ultimately come together as an integrated system. Critically, those components must:

1. *Formalize the roles and responsibilities of the senior leadership team* as champions of both the strategy and the breakthrough innovation teams set up to carry it out

2. *Set up an organizational model* that protects breakthrough innovation teams from the countervailing influences of the core

3. *Manage initiatives with an explore, envision, and discover process* so senior teams and innovation teams can learn their way to success together

We will describe the key elements of such a system in this chapter, but every company's circumstances are unique. Put another way, we can give you the key ingredients, but finding the right recipe is the work of you and your team.

The Roles—and Responsibilities—of the Senior Leadership Team

Senior leaders must be actively engaged in all the big decisions that determine a breakthrough effort's success or failure, championing the new strategy while leaning in to help the innovation team problem-solve when necessary. The ultimate responsibility for future-oriented initiatives cannot be delegated; that's why Ron Shaich, the founder and former CEO of the restaurant chains Au Bon Pain and Panera Bread liked to call himself the "discoverer in chief." "I think there are two big parts to any business, discovery and delivery," he told *Inc.* magazine. "One of my most powerful roles as CEO is to protect discovery. . . . My job," he added, "is to get this company ready for the future."[3]

Doing that well requires a substantial commitment of time. A. G. Lafley of Procter & Gamble told us he would sit down monthly with his head of R&D and, "depending on the innovations or technologies involved, the right players from the functions, P&G Ventures, and in some cases, the businesses. Then we would review the technologies, new products, and business model innovations we were developing and testing. The main point here," he added, is that "the CEO is de facto the CIO/Chief Innovation Officer in any company where innovation is a critical strategy to drive growth and value creation."[4]

The leaders of Boeing's Horizon X and Boeing NeXt innovation organizations meet monthly with Boeing's CEO, CFO, and Chief Technology Officer. As Boeing NeXt VP and general manager Steve Nordlund told us at an annual Innosight CEO Summit, "We don't present charts at these meetings. We have dialogue; we talk and pivot and learn."[5]

Governance

The first job of the senior leadership team is to design a governance system that will allow them to manage the implementation of the strategy as efficiently as possible, given all the competing demands on their time and attention.

It's best to aim for a minimally viable bureaucracy. Though you should establish clear rules for getting approvals, which will help avoid chaos and ensure adherence to the strategy, too much process bogs things down. Importantly, you should ensure that the breakthrough innovation teams report directly to senior

Example of New Growth Governance System

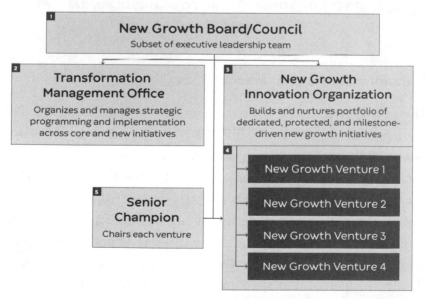

Design your organization to match the specifics of your strategy and your circumstance, but be sure to account for these five roles: (1) a senior governance board with accountability for the overall strategy, (2) a transformation management office to oversee day-to-day implementation, (3) a new growth organization (4) to nurture new growth ventures, and (5) senior champions to help shape each venture leadership and retain autonomy from the core business. Without this separation, disputes will inevitably arise. If senior leaders don't support the innovation teams, the core business will always win, sapping the new initiatives of their unique attributes and hence their breakthrough potential. Though maintaining autonomy may be relatively easy in the early days, once a new venture starts to attain scale it will become more threatening to the core and the fortitude of your governance model will be tested.

Often the senior leaders we work with create a "New Growth Board" or "New Growth Council" to oversee new growth initiatives. These are made up of a subset of key senior leaders (for example, the CEO, CFO, head of strategy, head of business development, head of R&D, and an expert outsider). As a senior champion, each will likely spearhead or sponsor one or more strategic initiatives germane to their expertise and passions, much as the partners at venture firms serve on the boards of several portfolio companies.

Transformation Management Office

The new growth board oversees everything, but the day to day management of this work should be administered by what we often call the transformation management office (TMO), which is usually led by a senior executive (typically the chief strategy officer or the COO), and staffed by a small group of full-time employees who have deep knowledge of the organization and are able to think beyond its conventional approaches and habits. Like a program management office (PMO) within established businesses, the TMO ensures that new initiatives have the resources they need, coordinates support for outside-the-core efforts from functions in the core, and makes sure that key metrics are achieved and milestones are met on time.

Master Plan

The TMO organizes and oversees a master plan, a living document that organizes all of the major tasks or activities related to the implementation of the strategy in one place, serving as both a roadmap and a dashboard that helps determine whether it is on or off track. This picks up from the walk back in phase two, in which the future state is reverse-engineered into a set of initiatives in the innovation portfolio. Similar to any simple work plan, the master plan breaks those initiatives (both outside the core and within it) down into chartered workstreams, with clear objectives, scopes, activities, timelines, and resourcing, covering both budgets and people.

Funding

Funding for core initiatives is relatively straightforward, as they won't require much in the way of new people, systems, and capabilities, and their business models are well understood. Funding for breakthrough initiatives should be ringfenced and protected at first (as specified in the investment portfolio), and then, as an initiative begins to mature, strictly metered to manage risk, ensuring that you're not investing too much or too long in any given idea before you're confident it's on a path to success. As we've seen, each Janssen initiative was only funded through its next milestone and then either closed down or accelerated.

Very few people are willing to admit defeat, but with breakthrough innovation work, the likelihood is that many of your projects won't ultimately succeed. Senior leaders should remind the teams that *what did you learn?* is as important a question as *what did you achieve?* As with venture capital, it's a portfolio game; pivot ventures when they need to pivot, and shut them down and reallocate their capital when they aren't panning out.

The Organizational Model for New Growth Innovation Teams

Before you get too far into the planning and execution of an initiative, you should bring in the people who will own it going forward. Look for a leader, like Janssen's Ben Wiegand, who has relevant domain expertise, general management skills, and entrepreneurial ability—the equivalent of a startup CEO—and team members who can play multiple roles.

Teams and Talent

Your new growth innovation teams should be small at first and staffed with cross-functional, co-located, and fully allocated (or nearly fully allocated) personnel.

> It is better by far to have two people on a new venture at a 100 percent allocation than ten people at 40 percent.

Don Sheets, a Dow Corning executive who founded a disruptive internal startup called Xiameter that became a major part of Dow Corning's business, looked for team members who had functional expertise and were good team players, but who were also "the-willing-to-stick-their-necks-out people." He knew he needed to build a fast-paced and entrepreneurial culture, so when he interviewed people he liked, he would offer them the job on the spot as a means of confirming they were comfortable making quick decisions.[6]

While the teams are small, you should expect them—and empower them—to tap into the functional prowess of the core business to access capabilities when they need them. And, of course, they should benefit from active and engaged senior sponsorship.

One of the trickier aspects of team design is the need to realign performance metrics and incentives. New efforts can be replete with uncertainty. You want to entice top talent with an entrepreneurial bent who aren't overly deterred by risk. You need to offer them some degree of upside for their participation, but it has to work in a corporate context with relatively rigid human resources guidelines. Senior HR leaders need to craft a talent management system with incentive packages that don't constrain the strategy but propel it. For example, they should spell out the career path benefits that will come from the demonstration of good judgment and right behaviors, even if projects ultimately fail through no fault of their own.

Wiegand negotiates those dynamics by a focus on personal mission. "We look for people with a true passion for our vision," he told us.

> They need to have a personal connection to what we're trying to do; it has to be part of what defines them as individuals. We would never succeed with people who are only partially committed, or who are in this because they find it interesting, or hope to use it to advance their careers. We look for people who see this as their opportunity to make a real difference, to build a legacy—because then they remain focused on the right things. I personally interview every applicant to the team to test for this—and across all of the offers we've made by now we haven't lost one, because we pick the people who are truly invested in what we're trying to do.[7]

Incubator Designs

In the early days of new growth strategies, your breakthrough innovation teams should be organized under an umbrella that is much like a start-up incubator, with dedicated teams vying for escalating rounds of funding as they build out and derisk their ideas.

Different types of incubator designs fit different stages of innovation development. Roy Davis, who was president of Johnson & Johnson's Development Corporation between 2008 and 2012, uses a hospital metaphor to describe the roles of distinct but linked innovation organizations: "Early stage projects, that aren't yet really businesses and have major assumptions to test, need something like a 'neonatal ward,' where there are specialized tools, a lot of support, and careful attention to nurture them to health. More mature projects, with early revenues but not yet at scale, can move to something like a 'pediatric ward,' where they'll receive a lot more attention than they would in the general hospital."[8]

Boeing created two linked organizations for its breakthrough efforts: Horizon X is responsible for seeding and shaping nascent beyond-the-core-businesses that focus on futuristic technologies like hybrid electric jets and autonomous flying taxis, while Boeing NeXt manages them once they have attained revenue but are not yet ready to stand on their own alongside or within Boeing's core businesses. As Logan Jones, vice president of Horizon X, put it, "Our job is to look over the horizon and do two things. One is to find ways to disrupt our company and ourselves before others do, and the other is to build a bridge to where innovation is maturing at a pace that big scaled enterprises aren't naturally attuned to."

Though some core processes and values may be non-negotiable, breakthrough innovation teams should be given as much freedom as possible to develop key processes like budgets and hiring, as well as rules, norms, and metrics that reflect their own unique missions. As Boeing's Jones put it, "the concept and structure of Horizon X came from failing. We had a sub-optimized innovation organization for years before Horizon X and NeXt existed and I was a proud leader of it. The problem was that it was buried within a business unit." Horizon X was set up as a separate limited liability corporation to isolate its risks and liabilities

Dual Transformation

Many visionary future-back strategies call for both a repositioning of your current businesses and the creation of a new,
beyond-the-core effort. To manage that, Innosight developed the concept of dual transformation, in which the core
and new growth business are managed as both distinct and
linked transformations, rather than as one monolithic effort. As noted earlier, this is covered in detail in the book
Dual Transformation.

Transformation A is what you do in your core business to
maximize its resilience into the future while generating sufficient cash to pay for new investments. Transformation B is
your new growth platform, whether acquired or developed
organically—or, most commonly, as a mix of the two. Leading,

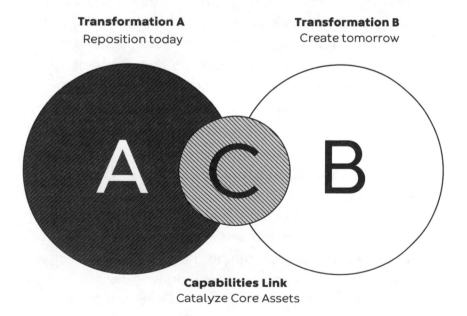

Transformation A
Reposition today

Transformation B
Create tomorrow

Capabilities Link
Catalyze Core Assets

organizing for, and executing B is a primary focus of this chapter, given how foundational it is to the successful implementation of visionary strategies.

The dual transformation model is designed to give B initiatives the autonomy they need to discover their own business models and develop appropriate rules, norms, and metrics. They should be connected enough to the core (via C, the Capabilities Link) to selectively leverage its capabilities while funneling newly developed capabilities back to it when appropriate. This is a difficult balance to strike, and it requires the active engagement of senior leadership. One useful mechanism to manage the balance is what we call exchange teams—small units empowered to arbitrate sticky issues, like how to approach customers for the new business who are still being served by the old.

A classic example of the dual transformation model comes from our colleague Clark Gilbert's experience as CEO of the *Deseret News*, a leading newspaper in Utah. As its leaders stared down the disruption presented by the rise of online media, they had to make some existential choices. While online media presented new opportunities, none were as profitable as the newspaper, even as its growth declined.

Gilbert's solution was to modernize the newspaper, leveraging the best digital tools he could get his hands on to bring it online, while pulling separate online ventures out of it (for example, entertainment guides) and developing them independently. Gilbert himself adjudicated disputes between the two groups, leveraging the newspaper's content to power the new ventures while channeling the digital tools and capabilities that the new ventures developed back to the newspaper.

from the rest of Boeing. Reporting directly to senior management allows its leaders to "get decisions made and move out with velocity." All of that was accomplished, Jones quipped, "through that less than sexy mission of governance, process, and structuring."[9]

Setting Up the Right Process

Beyond-the-core initiatives must be highly disciplined, but in a different way than those in the core. You cannot default to a present-forward mode; there are simply too many risks and unknowns in your new business model, calling for an emergent, test-and-learn approach. Both the senior team and the innovation teams should approach implementation as a learning process, embracing productive iteration and continually deepening and strengthening the abiding vision.

Creative problem solving and a discovery-driven approach to project planning are critical skills at this stage. Senior leaders and new growth teams should employ an innovation process that systematically identifies the assumptions most critical to the success of their proposition and then tests them in a targeted and orderly manner to prove or disprove their viability (and by extension the viability of the new initiative).

There are well-developed methodologies to guide this sort of work, such as Rita McGrath and Ian McMillian's Discovery-Driven Planning, materials produced by the Lean Startup movement, and the Innosight toolkit for accelerating innovative initiatives, laid out by our colleague Scott Anthony in his book *The First Mile*.[10] While innovation teams test assumptions related to their specific initiatives, the senior team should use the explore–envision–discover mentality to interrogate the direction and viability of the overall strategic program. As innovation teams learn and pivot, changing elements of their business model as it comes into contact with their customers, senior teams should do the same, adjusting the overall vision narrative and changing elements of the strategy as it comes into contact with the future. This learning orientation helps limit risk. Implicit in it, again, is the willingness to end projects that aren't working. In fact, in order to weed out the weakest initiatives, we find that it's advantageous to ask proactive questions like, *Why shouldn't we kill this venture?*

Step 2: Implementing Your Strategy

The work of breakthrough innovation can be likened to a quest. Although some breakthrough initiatives can take a decade or more to travel from the drawing board or the laboratory to scale, most take shape within a three-year span. In our experience, creating a vision, developing a future-back strategy, programming the strategy, and preparing your organization to launch it should take up year one. Then it's time for implementation, which takes you into year two and beyond.

As your pilot initiatives get off the ground, your immediate goal is to put points on the board by making progress on early-stage milestones, proving key assumptions, and achieving some quick wins. It's also critical to enact changes in your core business to create the cash flow that will be needed when it's time to ramp those initiatives up. In complex, multidivisional enterprises, the future-back strategy should cascade down to business units and even product lines as each develops its own future-back position in line with the new vision.

In year three and beyond, you begin to scale where you can, while making necessary adjustments to your systems to make sure that your changes to it stick. Your new strategy should increasingly be seen as *the* strategy.

You'll almost certainly face a series of crises in the course of your journey, as Mark and his coauthors describe in *Dual Transformation*.[11] One is a crisis of commitment. Any ambitious growth agenda will have its share of fumbles and false starts. There will be valley-of-death moments, when money is being spent but the turn toward accelerating revenue and profitability has yet to be seen. Another is a crisis of conflict. As we've noted, when new business initiatives start to draw in more capital, they compete with the funding needs of core businesses and the knives come out. Leaders need to demonstrate a steadfast commitment to the new growth efforts, helping to guide and shape them while fending off challenges from skeptical and even hostile colleagues, boards of directors, and outsiders.

As for the initiatives themselves, most pass through three stages as they mature: incubation, acceleration, and transition (a process that Mark covers in detail in his book *Reinvent Your Business Model*).[12] Like Boeing, companies can set up organizations specifically designed for each stage.

The Typical Timeline for a New Growth Platform

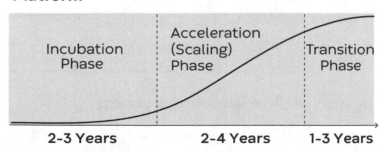

Incubation Phase	Acceleration (Scaling) Phase	Transition Phase
2-3 Years	2-4 Years	1-3 Years

During incubation, the assumptions most critical to the success of the business proposition are established and tested. In the acceleration phase you'll have much more knowledge relative to assumptions, so the focus is less on experimentation and more on setting up, refining, and standardizing repeatable processes, establishing the business rules that govern them, and defining the metrics that will chart their efficiency and profitability. Transition is when you determine whether the new business can be integrated into the core or if it should remain a separate unit.

As a set of general guidelines, a new business should be kept separate from the core when

- it calls for a significantly different set of business rules and accompanying metrics, which will evolve into significantly different norms

- it requires a distinct brand to fulfill its value proposition

- it tends to be disruptive to the core business model, making money with a lower margin, requiring new capabilities, or a different cost structure

On the other hand, it may be possible to reintegrate a new business into the core if

- its profit formula is substantially similar to that of the core business or provides greater unit margins

- it enhances the core brand in some significant fashion

- it can transform and improve the core

Nespresso: A Slow-Brewing Success

Today Nespresso is a household name, but its global success didn't happen overnight. Nestlé acquired the basic design for a single-serve home espresso maker in 1974 and introduced it in a few European markets in the early 1980s. Breakeven didn't come until 1995. In 2000, the same year the product debuted in North America, Nestlé changed

It Took Nestlé 25 Years to Learn How to Make Nespresso a Success

**1974 –1985
Incubation phase**
Nestlé bought design for single-serve espresso machine.

2000
Launch of successful boutique concept. Focus on sustainability.

**1995 –1999
Start-up phase**
Break-even reached in 1995. Expanded to a number of European markets. Ecommerce efforts expanded.

2015
$4.59 billion in revenue. 400 boutiques in 55 countries. Accounts for 4% of Nestlé's sales.

**1986-1994
Test and learn phase**
Introduced first machines and capsules. Gained scale in European markets. Nespresso Club launched.

2007
With a growth rate 5x the overall coffee industry, Nespresso is Nestlé's hottest brand.

2011
$3 billion in revenue. 10 million Nespresso Club members.

Note: Nespresso, of course, is an outlier; most initiatives don't take anywhere near this long to incubate and scale.

its marketing model and began to sell the product in "boutiques" in department stores. With its new elite ca-chet, Nespresso's sales increased by double digits year over year for nearly a decade. Hiring George Clooney as its spokesperson cemented its elite brand proposition even more. By 2015, Nespresso was a $4.5 billion global brand, and it continues to show mid-single-digit growth.

Setting Anchors

Given the time it takes new ventures to find their feet, you will inevitably be pushed to justify and re-justify the investments they require. As Hait puts it, "Leaders need to provide a constant activation energy to keep the program alive, or else it gets swallowed up. You work so hard to get the satellite in orbit, but it immediately starts to fall back to earth if you don't keep it up. The inertia of a big company will pull it back. Even if you succeed in setting up a separate group, others will constantly be poking at you. You need a steady drumbeat of success to stay ahead of the barbs, which is especially hard to do in areas that are unproven and inherently risky."[13]

That's why Hait stresses the criticality of near-term moves that bridge the objectives of both the new growth strategy and the core business—strategic choices we have come to call anchors. Anchors are moves—usually acquisitions or major partnerships—that in a single stroke make the strategy more real by bringing it heft and momentum. They generate early revenue, providing an additional funding mechanism for the new growth strategy, and bring an influx of talent and capabilities. The best anchors also create tangible value for the core business, generating goodwill and helping to keep skeptics at bay.

By 2018, the World Without Disease group's efforts in lung cancer had progressed to the point where J&J was ready to make a significant commitment, creating what they called the Lung Cancer Initiative and bringing in Dr. Avrum Spira, a physician/entrepreneur with expertise in the early detection and treatment of lung cancer, to head it up. Working in partnership with Ethicon, J&J's surgery business, Hait, Wiegand, and Spira quickly found their anchor, and in April of 2019 J&J acquired a Silicon Valley startup called Auris Health that had developed and recently launched the first robotic bronchoscope.

"One of the primary unmet needs that keeps us from effectively finding and treating lung cancer early, while it can still be cured, is that it is very hard to access suspicious lung lesions in order to confirm whether or not they're cancerous," Spira explains.[14] The Auris Monarch platform aims to change that by making it easier and more efficient for pulmonologists to reach deep into the lungs to sample suspicious lesions. As Hait puts it, "Colorectal cancer screening is well established with colonoscopy. Doctors use colonoscopes to simultaneously screen for polyps and sample them to make sure they're not cancer. Lung cancer has remained so deadly, in part, because we don't have analogous tools such as a *'pulmonoscope.'* We have recently started screening for suspicious nodules with Low Dose CT scans, but screening without effective means of confirmation has limited value. Now, with platforms like Monarch, we can complete the equation by more readily accessing tissue for biopsy through 'pulmonoscopy.'"[15]

The Monarch platform is an important step toward the larger vision of intercepting lung cancer, and it presents an opportunity for further development. For example, Spira's team is working with colleagues at Janssen to develop immuno-oncologic agents that can be delivered directly to the site of a tumor through the Monarch scope, theoretically increasing their efficacy.

Too many corporate startups fail because it takes them too long to make tangible progress. The Auris acquisition helped put the Lung Cancer Initiative on the map, giving it an identity as something more than an exciting idea. Best of all, it fit within Ethicon's future-back strategy as well. It was truly win-win, which helped ensure corporate support for the $3.4 billion acquisition.

Creating a vision, translating it into a future-back strategy, and then programming and implementing it is not a discrete event within a corporation's life. In a way, it *is* its life. The work is never done; visions and strategies must constantly be tested and adjusted. Meanwhile, there is always more future ahead of us, so newer ventures must be constantly begun. As such, future-back needs to become an organizational capability, led at the top, and permanently embedded in leadership mindsets, strategic planning processes, and organizational culture.

Chapters 6 and 7 will describe some of the ways you can institutionalize these capabilities and make them routine.

PART THREE

MAKING FUTURE-BACK REPEATABLE

Future-back thinking cannot be reserved for just the occasional offsite or even the heavy lift of our months-long vision and strategy development effort and the multiyear implementation process that follows. Once an enterprise reorients itself toward the portfolio of the future, it must ensure that its next generation of leaders continues to lead from the future. Boards must hire new CEOs who are aligned with the company's vision, and leadership development efforts are needed within the organization to ensure that the up-and-coming executives who will run the next set of initiatives—and ultimately the enterprise as a whole—know how to think, plan, and learn continuously. Leaders and managers at every level can also help to drive future-back thinking and make it a way of life. This doesn't mean that you must change your whole way of being. As noted earlier, present-forward thinking and processes will suffice for as much as 90 percent of your time. But to ensure a sustainable future, you must also spend time immersed in a different mindset—exploring, envisioning, and re-envisioning what is to come.

Of course, some leaders (the head of strategy, for example) will spend more time in the future; others (like the head of quality, for example) will spend much less. But all of them must carve out and preserve that time as individuals, as subgroups, and as a leadership team. Unconstrained by the distractions of the here and now, you must explore, envision, and discover, thinking from both the present forward and the future back as circumstances require.

The great strength of organizations is that they standardize processes and make them repeatable. As intuitive and imaginative as it is, future-back thinking can be institutionalized up to a point—both as a capability leaders must develop in themselves and one that should be encouraged and actively developed across the entire organization.

———————

Chapter 6

INFUSING FUTURE-BACK THINKING INTO LEADERSHIP TEAMS

The problems we face today come at us so fast and are so complex, that we need groups of talented people to tackle them, led by gifted leaders, or even teams of leaders.

—Warren Bennis

Making time for long-view thinking • "The prime ingredient in these decisions is judgment" • Toward a new
leadership framework • Resources talk • King Arthur,
CEO of Britain • The chemistry to dance • The board as
catalyst to visionary thinking • A recipe can't cook your
dinner

We've written about the new way of thinking that future-back leadership requires. But how does that work in practice in a large organization? In this chapter, we present a new framework for enterprise leadership that balances future-back and present-forward thinking.

A typical multinational organization is comprised of scores of business units, some of them in different industries and markets, operating in dozens of countries. With so many balls in the air, it's hard for leaders to carve out time or mindshare to think about and plan for the long term of the whole organization. Further, they tend to delegate their thinking about future technologies, products, businesses, and overall growth to their R&D organization, and appoint chief innovation officers to run their internal innovation or ventures organizations. This generally works well when it comes to long-term enhancements to the core and the development of close-in adjacencies, which don't require a different business model, a new set of people and competencies, or fundamentally different organizational capabilities to carry out. But as we've seen, it is a recipe for failure when it comes to the creation and management of discontinuous, beyond-the-core, white space plays. We would argue that enterprise leaders need to delegate more of their routine management tasks than they currently do so they can take a greater share of the burden of long-view thinking onto themselves. No matter how good the chief innovation officer may be, no matter how creative and entrepreneurial an innovation team, they cannot successfully create new market growth for an organization unless the leadership team is directly involved in their work, guiding them with their long-term vision and strategy, helping them create the right processes move their ventures forward, and protecting them from competition from the core.

> Without sufficient high-level attention, most breakthrough ventures won't even get off the ground.

We saw this happen not too long ago when a scientist in a consumer product company's R&D department developed a 3D-like printing technology to create one of its highly customized products on demand. Although there were still a few remaining technical hurdles to work through, the company's head of new growth platforms was excited about its disruptive implications—not just for manufacturing, but their whole value chain.

Potentially, a customer could walk into a store off the street, describe their needs, and walk out half an hour later with the product in hand. Such a model of onsite crafting would offer better and faster service to customers at a lower cost and provide them with even more personalization. And it wouldn't just be a boon for customers—instead of distributing their products via third parties, the company could own those stores themselves (or provide the same service on the internet), placing themselves squarely at the center of the competitive map of their industry.

Surely the idea was worth pursuing, at least on an exploratory level. We thought so. But our client's senior leaders hesitated. All they could see, it seemed, were its potential downsides—the remaining technical challenges (albeit imminently achievable, in the R&D team's view) and the threats to their existing factories, supply chains, and distribution channels, which might in time become obsolete. Without proof positive that the technology would work seamlessly and the new business model wouldn't destroy their old one without adding net growth, they refused to give it more than a very limited investment of people and dollars.

Had those top leaders regularly engaged in the kinds of strategic dialogues about enterprise vision and strategy we've described, they might have been able to envision a low-risk, low-cost way to prove or disprove this potentially breakthrough business's premises. Perhaps they could have started with a limited foothold test that targeted customers who would especially benefit from the added speed and personalization, and who weren't as well-served by the company's existing products. If initial results were promising, governance models like the ones we described in chapter 5 might have allowed them to grow the new business in tandem with their old, gradually shifting resources to it as it matured. Given the likelihood that a competitor would develop a similar technology in time, they might have inoculated themselves against their eventual disruption by disrupting themselves. Instead, the senior executives demanded proof of superior product and market performance, backed up by marketing data—data which by definition did not yet exist.

"Many of the important decisions we make," Jeff Bezos wrote in one of his annual letters to Amazon shareholders in 2005, "can be made with data. There is a right answer or a wrong answer, a better answer or a worse answer, and math tells us which is which." But sometimes, he added, "We have little or no historical data to guide us and proactive experimentation is impossible. . . . Though data, analysis, and math play a role, the prime ingredient in these decisions is judgment."[1] Our client's senior leaders needed to make a similar judgment call, but they didn't have to stake everything on their gut feelings. As real as the risks were, the concept could have been tested and managed in a risk-mitigated way. And its upside was potentially transformative.

It's not that those leaders' questions and doubts were unreasonable. In the best of all possible worlds, no one would ever have to compete with themselves, spend money on technologies that might not ultimately pan out, rely on business models that weaken over time, or see their capital investments become obsolete and lose their value. But that is not the world we live in.

Those leaders weren't averse to innovation per se. They created the group for new growth platforms that put the idea on the table, and their R&D department was highly respected and well-funded. But as with so many other leadership teams, they had brought a present-forward mindset to a future-back opportunity.

The opportunity is still there, waiting for someone else to pick it up, test it, modify it, and push it forward.

The Need for a Leadership Framework

Those leaders were not only using the wrong mindset; they were working within a model of enterprise leadership that was incomplete. The leadership framework depicted below matches up to the left brain/right brain, present-forward/future-back comparisons that we fleshed out in chapters 1 and 2.

The present-forward side lists the leadership capabilities needed for operating and executing the business—a profit-and-loss-oriented, relatively short-term perspective; mastery of straightforward, algorithmic processes; and a reliance on decision-making criteria turning primarily on financial data. That's where the leaders who were so skeptical of the 3-D printing opportunity were sitting.

The future-back side of the framework, in contrast, describes the more intuitive and creative set of leadership activities geared to exploring, envisioning, and discovering needed for efforts that are out-of-the-box and beyond-the-core. Its associated processes are iterative and driven by discussion and debate; decision-making turns on the insights gained as teams make the rounds of the learning loop.

Leadership Framework

Leaders must toggle between present-forward and future-back thinking

PRESENT-FORWARD	FUTURE-BACK
Leadership Focus: Near term Operations Execution	**Leadership Focus:** Long term Exploration Envisioning & discovery
Processes: Ordered Analytical Linear	**Processes:** Organic Creative Iterative
Decision Making Financial milestones Facts- and data-driven	**Decision Making** Learning milestones Assumptions-driven

Our client's leaders believed they were moving their organization forward, but by hewing so closely to the data-centric, operate-and-execute modality on the left side of the framework they were merely managing it—and potentially setting themselves up for a big failure down the road. Some leaders may know when to switch over to a different mindset instinctively, but most need to learn how and when to toggle over to the right—to become ambidextrous, to borrow a phrase from Michael Tushman and Charles A. O'Reilly III, and hence more innovative and creative.[2]

Business thinkers like Gary Hamel have proposed that top-down leadership and organizational creativity are inherently in conflict. Taking their cue from the internet, they argue that organizational charts should look more like networks than pyramids, with decision making distributed all the way out to their edges, where the most customer-facing employees are clustered. Innovation cannot be commanded and controlled, they declare; it must be allowed to emerge organically.[3] We agree that flatter and more egalitarian organizations are nimbler, have a more granular understanding of the markets and customers they serve, and are able to tap more creativity from their ranks than their more hierarchical peers. We also believe that the more decentralized and flatter an organization becomes, the more aligned and committed its top leaders must be in setting its overarching vision and the guiding growth principles that it entails.

Future-back Leaders Put the Enterprise First

The great industrial organizations of the nineteenth century developed silos of functions, each with its own distinct processes, practices, rules, and norms. Management itself, the art of organizing human systems so they add up to more than the sum of their parts, has evolved into more or less a science. There is a vast body of literature on teams and team-building. But as critical as leadership teams are, in most organizations they are not guided by the same kinds of explicit policies, procedures, and processes that functions and lines of business rely on. There's no lack of consensus on what the president of a business unit or a regional affiliate is supposed to deliver, or how a chief financial officer, a chief marketing officer, or the head of legal, procurement, HR, or manufacturing is supposed to operate, all the way up to the CEO.

But when the senior-most executives of a big, established business convene to make enterprise decisions, they're often loath to cede their functional or business-line roles as individuals. This can even happen with a CEO. A CFO who is promoted to CEO may continue to view the organization through a CFO's stringent financial mindset, just as a regional president may see it solely from the skewed perspective of the territory he or she is responsible for. When tasked to make critical resource allocation decisions for the enterprise as a whole, they might act to protect the interests of their old fiefdoms instead.

When we asked Udit Batra, the CEO of MilliporeSigma, a multinational life science business that is the product of a recent merger, how he persuades the heads of his newly blended business units to put the interests of the enterprise ahead of their own, he answered, "I think resources talk. Ultimately capital allocation matters, and everything else is a game. That's one part. The second is truly getting their buy-in—with hope and fear, or logic and love pushing them in the direction that you feel is appropriate. You need both tactics. You have to free up resources, and you have to force people's hands. You have to force their hands and then you have to support them to do it."[4]

How can CEOs bring their own leadership teams into line? Most of their members have already mastered the left side of the framework, as it matches up to what they do in their individual roles. But moving them over to the right side as a team is much, much harder. Hope, fear, logic, and love, and the subtraction or addition of operating resources are powerful persuaders all, but they are not a structured and repeatable approach; which is to say, a set of guidelines governing the focus of activities, the processes employed, and the decision-making criteria that a leadership team must use, even as its individual members come and go. Creating a true team of leaders is perhaps the greatest challenge that a CEO faces.

Consider the legend of King Arthur. Arthur was the CEO of Britain, and he drew his leadership team from the ranks of lesser kings, dukes, marquises, counts, viscounts, barons, and knights who managed its subsidiary kingdoms and territories. Each was a paragon of heroic chivalry, but when Arthur called them into council, they treated one another as rivals instead of peers, and very little got done. So Arthur ordered his carpenters to fashion a round table and a set of chairs, in order that, in the words of the Norman poet Robert Wace, "their chairs should be high alike, their service equal, and none before or after his comrade."[5]

Henceforth, things were different. When they were at home or off pursuing their quests, the Knights of the Round Table looked after their individual responsibilities. But when they went to Camelot, they conducted the business of state. The round table was the physical representation of the leadership framework that allowed them to become more than the sum of their parts.

Of course, these knights were fictional, but their story is a useful parable. Successful teams, whether they are knights of the realm, athletes, superheroes, government leaders, or business executives, must contain a diversity of strengths while maintaining a unity of purpose. The chief executive's job is not to erase their members' differences but to array their strengths in the best possible way. To do that well, they must know which way of thinking and acting is best suited to solve which problems and ensure that their team knows when it is time to execute and when it is time to explore and discover, when it is time to parse data and when they must summon the courage to walk a tightrope without the net of certain knowledge.

> Successful future-back teams must know what they know, but also what they don't know and must learn.

And they must be conditioned to act on what's best for the organization as a whole. If a CEO struggles to focus his or her leadership team, as a recent white paper from the Center for Creative Leadership (CCL) put it, "on learning, thinking, and leading globally across the enterprise, not merely on their particular functional areas," then they will also struggle in the rest of their job. Many do. The CCL cited a recent global survey of senior executives it conducted in which 97 percent of the respondents agreed that the "increased effectiveness of my executive team will have a positive impact on organizational results," but only 18 percent of them rated their own teams as "very effective."[6] That's quite an indictment.

Lining Up Your Leadership Team

Just knowing a leadership challenge exists goes a long way toward resolving it. So does the discipline that comes out of the diverge/converge process of strategic dialogues. When a CEO ensures that his or her team members really listen to their peers and know they are being heard in turn, their teams are more able to reach alignment on answers to the biggest and hardest questions. When they're able to develop a common language to describe a common set of goals, they are better able to problem-solve, commit and allocate resources, and sponsor and govern.

Mike Leavitt, a leading management thinker and insurance executive who is a former governor and cabinet secretary, told us that when it comes to leadership teams, "having the adaptability to make changes is like having the chemistry to dance. It is an intuitive sense about one's next move. Great dancers feel a nudge on the back or a dip of the shoulder and they know what that means. Great teams develop that kind of chemistry. Unless all the members are dancing toward the same objective, it doesn't happen. Great teams collaborate. It's a continual process of iteration in which people are willing to have disagreements that tease out differences and allow them to learn from each other."[7]

There is no one right way to build such a team, but it's mandatory that, in Jim Collins' words, the ultimate leader makes certain "the right people [are] on the bus (and the wrong people [are] off the bus)."[8] The CEO may need to change the composition of the team, adding or subtracting members as the circumstances dictate. Some may have to leave the organization. It's sad but true that knowing who to fire is as important a leadership capability as knowing who to hire and promote. When we asked enterprise leaders what their greatest regrets were, more than a few confessed it was that they waited too long to remove a senior executive who didn't add value, or who didn't contribute the right mindset to the team.

David Henshall, the CEO of the software company Citrix, told us he tends to include all of his senior-most executives in discussions about long-term planning and strategy. "But I've also cherry-picked a few individuals from around the organization that have unique knowledge, or who I believe can be high contributors to the dialogue. It's very narrow to believe that just the most senior people in the company have all the answers. But it's a balance, and finding out how to select those people without creating a situation where decision making gets muddied is a little bit of an art," he admitted.[9] R&D executives, designers, marketers who specialize in new product development, or senior executives from recently acquired companies can help catalyze the future-back thinking of a senior team that's overweighted with present-forward thinkers.

Terry Crimmins, the president of BAE Electronics Systems, told us that he divides his senior team into unequal parts, with the bulk of its members tasked with ongoing operations and a much smaller group given a charter to sit on the right-hand side of the leadership framework and focus on the future. "If you try to take the whole leadership team along for the ride when you're doing long-term strategy," he said, "forget it. But it's important to keep them all stitched together as a leading team as well. If you don't integrate that team back together on a routine basis, they become misaligned."[10]

People who are innately future-back or present-forward thinkers may not only have very different cognitive styles; they may feel uncomfortable or even threatened by their opposites. "Each side feels differently than the other," Bob Rivers, CEO of the Boston-based Eastern Bank, reflected when we showed him our leadership framework.

> The words I would use around the left side of the framework are *serious*, *disciplined*, and *self-critical*. The right side feels very different to me. Its emotions are *aspiration*, *optimism*, *risk orientation*, or, what I like more, *risk-taking*. Each side must appreciate and value the other, even if, innately, they don't embrace them. Both sides may feel fear when they look at each other. But the CEO has to be comfortable on both sides. If you, as the CEO, don't have an optimism about the future and a willingness to take risks, an aspiration, a sense that something's greater—if you can't play out there as the CEO, then this whole thing is dead.[11]

In a similar vein, Chris Chadwick, the now retired leader of Boeing Defense Systems, observed that "good leaders must be able to think from right to left," meaning from the future-back side of the framework, where a future-facing plan is envisioned, to the present-forward side, where the first stake is driven into the ground and an initiative is deployed.[12]

How does one develop that ability? Early on in these pages, we said that "if you want to change what you're doing, you have to first change the way you think." This is true when it comes to intentional processes, but when the goal is to change the way one leads, sometimes the opposite is the case. As the leadership and organizational behavior professor Herminia Ibarra has noted, "People change their minds by first changing their behavior. Mind-sets are very difficult to change because changing requires experience in what we are least apt to do. The only way to think like a leader," she continues, "is to first act. . . . Those freshly challenging experiences and their outcomes will transform the habitual actions and thoughts that currently define your limits."[13]

Ultimately, the secret to lining up a well-functioning leadership team that can think from right to left is to ensure that you spend enough time doing just that, individually and together.

> Just as there are annual budget reviews, you should establish quarterly future-back reviews—one- to two-day retreats in which senior leaders convene to revisit their vision and strategy, review the progress that their innovation teams are making, and further their own learning.

Obviously the frequency and duration of these reviews will vary depending upon your company's circumstances, but the key is to maintain a disciplined cadence of these kinds of conversations. As you and your colleagues grow more comfortable with future-back thinking, it will become second nature.

How Boards Can Enable Future-back Thinking

One refrain that emerged in nearly all our conversations with leaders is the positive role boards of directors can play in encouraging executives to take a longer view. Boards of directors have a fiduciary duty to serve as guardians of an organization's future; as such they can help ensure that its leaders don't neglect the right side of the leadership framework. Beyond simply hiring a new CEO who is not glued to its left side, they can press an incumbent CEO to spend more time on the right with his or her teams. As Bob Rivers put it, "Boards have a longer time horizon as a unit than CEOs do; the average retirement age now is seventy-five. They're typically going to be sitting there, call it ten years longer than the CEO. Most directors have an itch about the future that they need to scratch."[14]

Sandi Peterson, who sits on Microsoft's board, took up this theme as well. "I don't think the board's role is to set vision," she said. "I think its role is to be a catalyst to ensure that the company and the leadership of the company is setting the right vision and being bold enough, thoughtful enough about that. The board is not close enough to the day-to-day, the competitive landscape, and the customers to be the ones who say: 'This is the vision,'" she continued. "But they can push the leadership team to think bigger and bolder than they have been, or in some cases the opposite. . . . The board doesn't own the vision, but it owns ensuring that it happens, that there's enough conversation about it, and that teams are being pushed hard enough on how to think about it."[15]

"The way I look at my role as a board member," Rich Bane, a director of Eastern Bank, told us, "is not to be focused on the day-to-day. The board should be thinking about the bigger picture every day. The board has to say, 'We believe in innovation, we believe in the future. We believe in the need to think long-term.'"[16]

The board should not let itself be steered by the CEO, which is something that happens far too often; it's important that it develop its own perspective, and it should have a broad understanding of the organization's broader culture. To ensure that it does, its members must interact with lower-level executives when they can. If their own meetings are too focused on compliance and governance matters, that should raise a red flag. "Executive sessions without any members of management in attendance, including the CEO, is a really good thing to do," Peterson observed. "If it's a well-run, functioning team of board members, they should be able to raise those high-level issues."[17]

Boards have a big role to play in ensuring that an organization's new leader builds on the progress that its old one made—or, conversely, that a new leader sets a different vision and leads the organization in a better direction, if that is what's called for. If a leader is too focused on the short term, the board can press him or her to take a longer view. If the board itself has been exclusively focused on governance and operations, it needs to expand its own thinking.

Of course, not all boards are bastions of visionary thinking; most directors were shaped in their own careers by present-forward incentives and systems, and they are as vulnerable to short-term cognitive biases as the leaders of the companies they oversee. Most expect CEOs to keep share prices rising and to avoid making ambitious bets on beyond-the-core initiatives that are too risky, as indeed they should.

But a visionary CEO who has a sound and actionable plan for a different future can often enlist even a conservative board as an ally. As Chris Chadwick told us:

> For 90 percent, even 99 percent of the organization, my message was, "Here's the path you're on and here's what I need

you to do and why." But when I went to the board, my message was also, "Here's where we're going to go in the long term and how we're going to introduce new elements into our business." By presenting both our present and our future to them, I was better able to open their eyes to both the quarter-to-quarter reporting-to-the-street elements and our vision. In other words, I never forgot I had a day job, which was to deliver results. But I could also make them see that the future was changing drastically, even if it was twenty years out.

The cool thing about briefing the board was that I learned to give them the benefit of the doubt. When I first started talking about my future-back view of digital transformation, the board would ask very tough questions. We are a very manufacturing-heavy company, after all. But with the right answers, they would begin to buy into it and embrace it. So yes, you can get alignment with the chairman and the board. And then of course, it's not enough to just *think* future-back. You need to slowly institutionalize that change inside the organization, so that when the next person comes along to fill your role, it's difficult for things to just wholesale default to the way they used to be. You're building in new foundations as you go that embrace that new way of thinking and what it has brought to the business.[18]

At the end of the day, the leadership framework is just that—a schematic representation of the kinds of thinking and decision-making processes a senior team needs to master before it can manage an enterprise. Just as a map can't transport you to your destination and a recipe can't cook your dinner, the framework is not an operating system. Leaders and their teams must learn to stretch themselves, to think in ways that may be hard for them and will likely feel unnatural to some.

What Senior Leadership Teams Need to Successfully Drive Long-Term Growth

- A diversity of strengths

- A unity of purpose, guided by a shared vision for the enterprise as a whole

- The understanding that successful enterprise leadership is as much about exploring and envisioning as executing and operating

- The wisdom to know which capability is called for and the ability to balance them when more than one is required at the same time

- A willingness on the part of its members to change their behavior, even if they're not yet ready to change their minds

- The guidance of a strong, independent board and a willingness to collaborate with it

But a map can help you find your way when you're lost and a recipe can help you turn a list of ingredients into a meal. Simply having the leadership framework and a five- to ten-year or longer growth horizon can make you more conscious of the need to do those difficult things.

In chapter 7, we will describe some of the ways you can embed future-back thinking in your organization.

Chapter 7

INFUSING FUTURE-BACK THINKING INTO YOUR ORGANIZATION

What we've done to encourage
innovation is make it ordinary.

—Craig Wynett

Steering the ship of the navy • Continuity of vision • Remove "single points of failure" • "Boards are the stewards of the company's future" • "Strategy, innovation, and leadership can be learned" • Screening for future-back leaders • Building a learning culture • Finding a higher purpose

---

When this book was still in its very early stages, we visited Admiral James Stavridis at the Fletcher School of Law and Diplomacy at Tufts University, where he was dean, and shared some of our thinking with him. Over the course of Stavridis's thirty-seven-year military career, he rose to commander, US Southern Command; commander, US European Command; and NATO Supreme Allied Commander Europe. He spoke frankly about his struggles to steer the ship of the US Navy in a different direction.

"The navy is an inherently hierarchical organization," he said, "and it prides itself on the orderly execution of business in the operational sense of the word. When the military wants to improve, it tends to do repetitive training to get better. But the seductive and dangerous quality of repetitive training is that it works. So, it's hard for the military to acknowledge the kinds of jump shifts that must occur because of new technologies and new situations."[1]

When Stavridis turned his lens on himself, he was unsparing:

Where I failed was at the US Southern Command. I went down there full of hubris. I was a new, very young four-star officer. I said, "I know what's going on here. This is Latin America. We're not going to go to war. We're not going to invade Venezuela or Cuba or Mexico. Our challenges are different than warfare, which is what our organization is optimized for. Our role is counter-narcotics, disaster relief and preparedness, medical diplomacy, humanitarian operations." So, I got out a piece of paper, sketched out my new staff structure, called in my senior team, handed out copies, and said, "What do you think?" They all said, "Wow, that looks great, Admiral." Then we did a few day-long workshops and we implemented it.

But then after three years I got reassigned to be the commander of NATO, and my successor came in. Within three months, it was right back where it was. As we always say in the military, "No good idea survives the change in command." What we discovered is that the brilliant mind theory of innovation is a lousy way to innovate. Innovation needs that spark, but it needs buy-in and it needs time to inculcate it. You need to build the culture and make the argument and tell the stories. You need to carve out the time to do it right.

In this chapter we will look at how to do future-back thinking, and the innovative mindset that it enables, right—and how to inculcate it in the people and processes of organizations. As with so much else, it begins with vision and must be led from the top.

Continuity of Vision

A powerful vision encompasses a galvanizing aspiration to achieve a grand purpose ("to change the trajectory of health for

humanity, we will accelerate the development of healthcare solutions that eliminate disease") and a clear set of concrete goals
that energizes and aligns employees, customers, and investors
alike ("a *World Without Disease* will be focused on innovative
drugs, but also on whatever else it will take to realize the vision—
be it consumer health products, medical devices, or digital
therapeutics").[2]

Effective future-back leaders communicate the vision relentlessly, across the organization and outside it, ensuring that every
employee understands it and knows how they can contribute to
it themselves. They prepare employees and investors for the
changes that will come and celebrate and recognize the efforts
that contribute to the vision's success. As A. G. Lafley put it to us, "I
believe in sharp thinking and clear communication to move a
large, complex business ahead and its organization to constructive and productive action. I cannot overemphasize the importance of CEO leadership communication regarding innovation
and the specific business unit strategy choices that go with it."[3]
They also continuously and carefully cultivate and shape the
vision to keep it relevant, watching the initiatives that grow out
of it closely to be certain they are giving them all they need to
flourish.

But at the same time, Admiral Stavridis's anecdote illustrates
the challenges of what Jim Collins called "the genius with a thousand helpers" leadership model, in which a charismatic leader
embodies the vision and the direction of an organization but is
either unwilling or unable to teach others how to do what they do
so well.[4] Think of Akio Morita, who built Sony from a tiny radio
repair business into a global giant by serially disrupting it but
whose successors struggled for years just to keep the organization
in the black, or Microsoft, which, despite experiencing incredible
sales growth after Bill Gates turned it over to Steve Ballmer, missed
opportunity after opportunity to dominate new technologies. How
can an organization ensure that its future-back initiatives will

survive the visionary leaders and teams who conceived them and set them into motion?

In August, 2019 Jack Dorsey, the leader and founder of Twitter and Square, gave a talk at Innosight's annual CEO summit in which he emphasized the importance of vision, how a jobs-to-be-done approach can ensure that an organization retains its focus on its customers' deepest needs, and, critically, the danger of overdependence on a single leader. "I don't want to build a company that's dependent upon any one person, including me," he said. "I think if I have to make a decision there's actually something wrong with the organizational structure, because I'm not the closest to the customer."

And then he zeroed in on the unacceptable risk of having a "single point of failure":

> My job is threefold: Number one, making sure that we have an amazing team dynamic, that we are together building a dynamic that is healthy, that contributes to our strength, and that is challenging in a way that makes us better.
>
> Job number two is that decisions are being made in the context of who we serve, in the context of our customers, of technological, social and cultural trends, and of our competition.
>
> And then the third job is just raising the bar on what we thought was possible. I want to avoid creating a dependency upon me or our current leaders, because to do that is to have a single point of failure. I want to build a company like Disney, that has survived the death of its founder and continues to carry on the same mindsets, the same drive to build an ecosystem of functions and products that are not dependent on any one person being there for the rest of their lives. I want a decision-making framework,

and a product-planning framework that removes single points of failure.[5]

Boards and CEO Succession

If you sit on a board of directors, we hope chapter 6 convinced you that the future-back framework we prescribe applies to you no less than it does to the people who occupy the C-suites you oversee. As we discussed, boards are chartered to protect and champion the future. As such, they can help in the work to institutionalize future-back thinking, ensuring that it remains an enduring organizational capability.

A.G. Lafley recognized this when he created an upstream innovation group within P&G's board of directors that he calls the Innovation and Technology Committee. There are two ways, he told us, that the committee adds value: First, it helps the board get comfortable with a really long-term view of innovation, "the fact that some of the things we're going to take a run at are going to take ten or fifteen or more years to develop. The foam that is the basis of P&G's Always and Whisper feminine care products, for example, began its development process in an R&D lab in the 1990s." As he tells it,

> We didn't have prototypes until ten years later. And we didn't have the first test product in the market for fifteen years. Even then, we hadn't figured out a margin that was really going to make sense. We introduced it as a new brand in Germany and it didn't work. Then we went back and reintroduced it as an ultra-premium line in the category-leading Always brand so that we could generate more trials and have a chance at economic viability. I mention this because I think getting the board to understand that we were going to

be placing some long-term bets meant that they would be more open to, "Hey, we're not going to maximize quarterly profits or annual profits because we're always going to be investing in innovation to create future businesses." That turns the conversation to "how much?" which is a much better discussion to have with them than one in which the question is whether you should invest on an on-going basis in innovation/technology breakthroughs at all. While some initiatives fail and need to be discontinued, turning off the investment process itself is death for innovation and future business growth.

The other thing that was really important is that we were thinking about board composition; we actively recruited for board members who were engaged constructively in innovation and technology, who were comfortable with the long-term investment and support required and the risks associated with innovation and technology bets. When a board is actively involved in innovation strategy and investment decisions, you can bring in CEOs with significant innovation experience in different industries. The board and I began to assess our business unit CEOs not just on their business and financial results but also on their strategy, innovation, and leadership—how they personally contributed to results in the short term and how they were positioning their businesses competitively for the longer term.

The pressures for short-term thinking are there, and I think it's really important for the board and the CEO to share a view about what's right for the long-term health of the business. I can't tell you how much the long-term matters. We were an unusual company—we thought about becoming 200 years old and when we get to 200, we'll think about being 210. The Innovation and Technology Committee and the board institutionalizes this best practice.[6]

Intuit's Scott Cook (one of those future-facing business leaders that Lafley recruited for his board) also had much to say about the positive synergies between CEOs and boards when we interviewed him. "The CEO needs to be thinking far, far into the future," he said. "And the board has to be a part of that. Its makeup is crucial, the schools of experience that its members represent. It sure helps when some have a history of creating or backing new businesses. They have to have been willing to learn from failure and stay the course, despite the pressure to deliver short-term results. Most of the examples of companies that do this successfully are founder-led, and that's no coincidence. It's much harder with established companies."[7]

It's tragic that an institution which in principle is meant to be a solution can so often be a part of the problem. In too many cases, CEOs' relationships with boards are incestuous. But truly strong and confident CEOs recruit collaborators rather than cronies. Collaborative board members must constantly, as Scott Cook put it,

> look in the mirror and ask themselves, 'Are we moving this company toward its demise or to its long-term success?' CEOs should ask them those questions too, and not be afraid to shame them when necessary. Boards are the stewards of the company's future. Your job as a board member is not to dump and run; it is to set the company up for success year after year. After all, how would you feel about your tenure as a university trustee if afterwards your school shut down? How would you feel as a church deacon if after your leadership the flock fled? You would think you betrayed your institution.[8]

The most direct influence a board has on a business's innovation culture is in its choice of its next CEO. Choosing a new CEO is not just an ultra-high-level human resources decision, or, like a sports franchise's efforts to sign the superstar players that score the most points and attract the most ticket-buyers, a way to improve an enterprise's brand and competitiveness. The CEO the board hires must be willing to develop a vision and have the leadership abilities to implement it. If the board believes that the current CEO had the right vision, then they must be careful to pick a new one who will sustain it. If they believe that a change in direction is called for, then they should hire a CEO who is willing to refresh and revise it.

If the board chooses a new leader from outside the organization who has a burning vision of what their new organization could become, the board can help them be more realistic about their time horizons as they learn about and acclimate to their new environment. Ideally, the new CEO will be an avid learner already.

In some organizations, the heir-apparent is identified years in advance and apprenticed by the current leader and board. We've talked to a number of leaders who see this as the best possible approach, but Sandi Peterson, who, as mentioned earlier, sits on Microsoft's board, strongly disagreed. "For lots of reasons," she told us, "people who are good Number Twos don't necessarily turn out to be great leaders.

"Boards should not let CEOs manage succession processes in the ways that they frequently do," she continued emphatically, "because of human nature. Frequently what happens is the person who ends up being advocated by the CEO has spent an immense amount of time managing up and making the CEO very happy. That creates a certain bias. The process needs to be owned more by the board." Echoing some of our future-back language, she added, "Boards need to spend time thinking about how the world is changing, what the business is going to look like in five years, and why that might be different than the last five years. They need to spend time thinking about their criteria for the next leader."[9]

Executive Development Programs

While the optimal CEO hire may be external, most of the C-suite denizens who make up an enterprise's leadership team rise through the ranks at one or more of their organization's business units. It's critical that the right people with the right skillsets are promoted. This is also true for the innovation teams that run new initiatives. Development programs and thoughtful mentorship can go a long way toward ensuring that there is a strong pipeline of up-and-coming future-back leaders.

Companies spend billions of dollars on leadership development programs (by one estimate, some $14 billion per year in the United States).[10] These run the gamut from one-and-done offsite workshops to classroom courses conducted in business schools; others provide high-potential executives with customized, on-the-job training and coaching. Giant corporations like GE, IBM, and P&G maintain virtual full-time universities for current and future leaders throughout their organizations.

Johnson & Johnson's Accelerate Enterprise Leadership (AEL) program has proven especially effective for developing the skills of leadership, innovation, and corporate entrepreneurship in a real-time, hands-on context. This eight-month program, designed for senior executive VPs nominated for global leadership roles, is unique in that it requires a significant investment of time outside of one's job. It's designed to foster an enterprise-wide, growth-oriented mindset while developing its participants' outside-in perspectives through facilitated team projects, residencies in global locations, and immersions in emerging markets.

In one year, for example, AEL tasked a group of participants to develop business ideas for William Hait's then-nascent World Without Disease initiative. To that end, they were dispatched in small teams to locations around the world, to meet with government health officials, hospital administrators, doctors, and patients. Then, after six months of coaching from executive mentors and outside experts, they presented their business plans to J&J's executive and management committees. Some received funding, and one of the participants opted to join the initiative full-time, making disease interception the focus of the next stage of her career.

AEL is just the tip of the iceberg of J&J's strategic human resources efforts, which provide team and individual coaching to existing executives and programs to accelerate the onboarding of newly hired or promoted ones, as well as targeted learning programs, based on case studies, for the benefit of members of the C-suite, including the CEO.

A. G. Lafley told us about a highly targeted leadership and strategy development program he ran with his highest-potential leaders and managers.

> We believed that strategy, innovation, and leadership could be learned and taught by a combination of successful practitioners and conceptual pioneers. I personally believe in three-person learning—that mastery only comes with first learning, then doing/practicing, and finally teaching others. I was personally committed to teaching and coaching the concepts and practices that I expected my future leaders to learn and master. In my experience, there are fewer innovators than there are operators, just as there are fewer strategists than there are operators. Having said that, in our organization, with our business model, we needed to develop a handful (or two) of "ambidextrous" leaders who could do it ALL—strategy, innovation, and inspirational leadership—well enough to manage large global businesses and potentially to lead the company as CEO. Fortunately, a few were able to develop the capabilities and skills and get the experience the results required.[11]

Screening Future Leaders

Senior leaders should screen for up-and-coming talent with an aptitude for the right-hand side of the leadership framework. One way to do this is to leverage the toolkit that Jeffrey H. Dyer, Hal Gregersen, and Clayton Christensen identified as "the innovator's DNA" in a *Harvard Business Review* article and follow-up book with the same title. It turns on five attributes that map to the right side of the leadership framework.[12] These are associating, questioning, observing, experimenting, and networking. People who have them should be actively sought out, encouraged, and mentored, as they will likely leave to pursue their entrepreneurial interests on their own if they are not given the right opportunities.

Associating is the ability to make unexpected creative connections among seemingly unrelated things, to cross-pollinate ideas by combining and recombining them. "Creativity is just connecting things," Steve Jobs wrote. "When you ask creative people how they did something, they feel a little guilty because they didn't really do it, they just saw something. It seemed obvious to them after a while. That's because they were able to connect experiences they've had and synthesize new things."[13]

Questioning is the penchant for following the unconventional, open-ended inquiries that comprise the essence of abductive reasoning to their sometimes counterintuitive answers, such as, *If we did this, what would happen?* In the HBR article that introduced the idea of the innovator's DNA, the authors cited the case of Michael Dell, who remembered asking himself why computers that were built from $600 of parts had to be priced at $3,000. The answer was, they didn't—and his discount computer business was born.

Business innovators closely observe the behaviors of customers, suppliers, and competitors. A. G. Lafley traveled the world to see how customers in different countries and cultures cleaned their homes and did their laundry. "Often the surprises that lead to new business ideas come from watching other people work and live their lives," Scott Cook has observed. Cook noticed that 50 percent of his customers for Quicken, the personal finance software he developed to target to individuals, were actually small businesses. The result was a new business: Quickbooks, an accounting software for small businesses, which eventually grew to twenty times the size of Quicken.[14]

Experimenting is using the world as a laboratory. People who see themselves as citizens of the world have a broader perspective than those who are tied to one place. They are more open to importing ideas and practices that might seem exotic at first glance, and they are more willing to export ideas that work in one place to another, adapting them as necessary. A study carried out by the authors of the innovator's DNA article revealed that the more countries an innovator has lived in, the more likely they are to leverage that experience to deliver new products, processes, and businesses. A. G. Lafley studied history in France in college and was the director of P&G's Asia operations before he became its global CEO. Unilever's former CEO, Paul Polman, who put sustainability at the heart of his enterprise vision, grew up in the Netherlands, considered joining the priesthood, and then completed his graduate work in economics and finance at the University of Cincinnati in the United States.

And finally, networking is the drive to test ideas by exposing them to peers and people from other walks of life. Business innovators are sponges for unfamiliar ideas; as such they seek out conferences and other venues to exchange and combine their ideas. The innovator's DNA article describes how Kent Bowen, the founding scientist of CPS technologies, hung a sign in every office that read: "The insights required to solve many of our most challenging problems come from outside our industry and scientific field. We must aggressively and proudly incorporate into our work findings and advances which were not invented here."[15]

Traditional metrics that assess future leaders tend to focus on the results they deliver in terms of dollars. Career paths should also be planned and assessed according to up-and-comers' entrepreneurial experiences and capacities. If younger executives avoid risky new ventures because they rightly fear that their failures may be held against them, then that is a systemic problem in your organization that must be addressed. As discussed earlier, up-and-comers must know they will be safe in the event of an unavoidable failure and have a reasonable expectation of receiving some upside in the form of salaries, bonuses, and promotions if a venture succeeds.

A Visionary Organization Learns, Adapts, and Grows

We have described the learning loop of explore, envision, and discover in the context of vision creation and strategy development and the pursuit of new business models and growth initiatives. But learning is much more than an executive tool to be trotted out only when it is needed to solve a particular problem; it is a way of being. Visionary organizations create structures that incentivize collaborative learning at every level. Ideally, they're populated with the avidly curious yet practical people who fit the description of Carol Dweck and Satya Nadella's "Learn-it-alls" we met in chapter 2.[16]

Mark studied with the late David Garvin at Harvard Business School and collaborated with him on a number of projects. "A learning organization," Garvin wrote in his classic book *Learning in Action*, "is an organization skilled at creating, acquiring, retaining, and transferring knowledge; and at purposefully modifying its behavior based on new knowledge and insights."[17]

The book is filled with detailed case studies based on his personal observations of the inner workings of a host of organizations and companies, from L.L. Bean to the US Army. In it, he laid out the systems and processes that maximize an organization's ability to gather and analyze intelligence from outside and draw lessons from within via postmortems and after-action reports and the discipline of systems analysis. Garvin's focus was not so much on the applied research carried out in R&D laboratories but on how organizations can translate knowledge of all kinds into better ways of operating. If profitability and productivity present a snapshot of a company's health at a given moment in time, he wrote, its ability to learn reflects on its capacity to correct and improve its operations, adapt to changing conditions, develop new ideas, and prosper over the long term. In that sense, learning is just as vital to present-forward as future-back thinking.

Organizations that seek to prioritize an ethos of continual learning, fostering a business culture that not only improves its existing offerings but continually develops transformative new ones, must provide settings that are psychologically safe for exploring, envisioning, and discovery. Streamlining approval processes for test-and-learn initiatives, empowering customer-facing middle-managers to make decisions, and tying compensation to innovation as well as profitability all make a difference.

"Employees," Garvin wrote, "must feel that the benefits of pursuing new approaches exceed the costs."[18] Successful learning organizations enforce norms that reward innovative thinking while at the same time legitimizing the making and surfacing of mistakes, so their causes can be corrected. No one should ever feel they are putting their job in jeopardy by trying to solve a problem or develop something new that might not pan out.

"One of the big things we have done at the leadership level," Microsoft's Satya Nadella told an interviewer, "is to focus on shared metrics. We make a distinction between what we call 'performance metrics' and 'power metrics.' Performance metrics are in-year revenue and profit and things of that nature. Power metrics are about future-year performance. They are leading indicators of future success."[19] As Gustavo Manso wrote in *The Journal of Finance*, "Innovation involves the exploration of new untested approaches that are likely to fail . . . the optimal incentive scheme that motivates innovation exhibits substantial tolerance (or even reward) for early failure and reward for long-term success."[20] The key is to recognize the path, and not just the immediate results.

There is a significant body of academic work on organizational learning, among them Peter Senge's books (most notably *The Fifth Discipline: The Art & Practice of the Learning Organization*[21]) and the research of Chris Argyris and Donald Schön, who introduced the concept of double-loop learning. While single-loop learning seeks to analyze causes and effects in the pursuit of optimization, double-loop learning goes deeper and asks reflexive questions about the *why* of a thing—not just, *"How can we improve this process or strategy?"* but *"Why do we do things this way?"* and even more to the point, *"How am I contributing to the problem?"*

Double-loop learners see beyond the orthodoxies that define the present-forward mindset. If they're self-critical, it is in the search of a better way. "Most people define learning too narrowly as mere 'problem-solving,'" Argyris writes, "so they focus on identifying and correcting errors in the external environment. Solving problems is important. But if learning is to persist, managers and employees must also look inward. They need to reflect critically on their own behavior, identify the ways they often inadvertently contribute to the organization's problems, and then change how they act."[22] Double-loop learners don't just get smarter, they get wiser. And they are more creative.

Carol Dweck has noted how the fear of being judged can inculcate a fixed mindset in which people believe talent is a quality they either have or don't. If people believe they are perceived to have talent, they may avoid risk-taking, lest they put their status into jeopardy, and refuse to collaborate, lest someone else get the credit for their collaboration. If they believe they are perceived as untalented, they may either give up or give way to resentment.

> **A growth mindset is the belief, actively ratified by management, that it's possible for anyone to learn, develop, and grow.**

"When entire companies embrace a growth mindset," Dweck writes, their employees "report feeling far more empowered and committed; they also receive far greater organizational support for collaboration and innovation. In contrast, people at primarily fixed-mindset companies report more of only one thing: cheating and deception among employees, presumably to gain advantage in the talent race."[23]

One of our Innosight colleagues related a conversation she had about framing with Harvard Business School's Amy Edmondson. When situations get heated, some leaders adopt a frame of "I'm right and you're wrong," and then attempt to convince, control, and overcome the other person, who is seen as an adversary. Efforts must be made to replace that frame with "I have a valuable point of view but I may be missing something." In this frame, the goal is to learn and problem-solve, and the other person is seen as a resource rather than an obstacle.

Building a Learning Culture

The learning that comes from constructive debate travels from the top down and the bottom up; it emerges from the give-and-take among an organization's senior leaders, its middle managers, and its rank-and-file. It is important to actively and intentionally create processes and structures, and most importantly a culture in which every voice is heard.

Ferdz dela Cruz, the former chief executive of Manilla Water, told us that both the incentive structures in his company and its mandatory retirement rules tend to keep his senior team focused on a time horizon just two to three years ahead. "Everybody says they care about the long-term, but in ten years, all of my direct reports will have retired," he said. "I think it's worth having the younger executives tell the senior executives what the future might look like. I have a reverse mentor who's one of our younger executives. We need to involve the millennials, the thirty-five to forty-year-old executives in our discussions. We are going to experience a big kink in our demographics, so we're trying to change the way we work, from how our office looks to the tools that we use, so that we are an environment for the next generation as well."[24]

"The CEO," Satya Nadella wrote in *Hit Refresh*, "is the curator of an organization's culture. Anything is possible for a company when its culture is about listening, learning, and harnessing individual passions and talents to the company's mission. Creating that kind of culture is my chief job as CEO. Inclusiveness," he continued, "will help us become open to learning about our own biases and changing our behaviors so we can tap into the collective power of everyone in the company" (the double loop). Key to that transition, he added, is "individual empowerment. We sometimes underestimate what we each can do to make things happen, and overestimate what others need to do for us."[25]

Andy Hill, the former CEO of Jarden Consumer Products, told us:

> One of the things I tried to instill in my organization is that nobody is smarter than the next person. On a given day, you

might be the smartest one in the room. But the next day? You're going to be in a different group and you're not going to be the smartest one. So, collaboration is important. For me, it was the thing that was probably the single most important cultural element in my organization. It helped us succeed when others couldn't, because I wouldn't allow a noncollaborative environment to exist. I rooted it out at every turn and when I found areas where people were not being collaborative, they didn't last in the organization long. I could go through fifty examples of people I fired because I knew they would never develop that collaborative cultural approach to the organization, to the people, and to the development of the business and the strategy.

If you're not aligned culturally, if you can't define what the culture is, what kind of culture it is that you expect people to operate within, it won't work. It can't work. With that said, diversity is one of the most important things you can have. The example I use is my CFO. He and I ran the company together, but he was the opposite of me from a personality standpoint. He would really get into the details; he'd sit and go through a fifty-page spreadsheet with two hundred lines on each spread. Me, I'm more big-picture, more people-oriented, more focused on results, what all of that is going to look like, than the numbers on the page. We were a great complement to each other. You should have people surrounding you that are different, that think about things differently. People that have come from different backgrounds, and done different things. Diversity on just about every axis. When we decide to do something, I want everybody to go do it. But I want very diverse points of view coming in before. You need to decide how your team needs to interact with itself from a cultural standpoint, and if you've got someone on the team that can't adapt to that, then they don't belong on it.[26]

Demographic diversity is important too—in the company as a whole, in its senior ranks, and on the board. More and more, it is not just a social virtue but a competitive advantage, because it ensures a better understanding of customers and a greater receptiveness to new ideas. "I'm a huge proponent of diversity on the board in all of its permutations," Sandi Petersen told us. "Geographic, business experience, gender, industry. It's hugely valuable. Since I've started being on boards, it literally used to be a bunch of retired CEOs and COOs. That's just not the case anymore, which is good. We still have a lot of work to do on ethnic diversity," she added, "But we're getting there."[27]

Having a Sense of Purpose

Until now, we've mostly written about vision in the actionable sense of the word. But when the task at hand is to change or sustain an organization's culture, the more abstract connotations of the words *vision* and *visionary* (those relating to grand purposes and reasons for being, also sometimes called a company's mission) come into play. Having a higher purpose is not strictly necessary for a business to succeed, but as countless studies have found, it can go a long way toward motivating its employees and stakeholders, and it helps in recruiting new talent. Paul Polman recognized that when he committed Unilever to an ambitious plan to double its revenues while at the same time reducing its negative impacts on the environment, improving the nutritional quality of its packaged foods, bettering the living conditions of the farmers and other workers in the developing world who supply its resources and work in its factories, and raising employees' pay and making its workforce more inclusive across the board.

It's best when the people in an organization are inspired by a set of shared goals and a sustaining sense of mission. An analysis conducted by Gallup of 49,928 business units across

192 organizations in thirty-four countries and forty-nine industries found a close correlation between missions and margins. The
more aligned employees are with a company's transcendent *what*
and *why*, the more they believe its stated values are reflected in their
workplaces; the higher their productivity; the stronger their connections with their customers; and the longer they are likely to stay
with the company.[28]

In 2019, Innosight sought to identify the twenty global companies that have achieved the highest-impact business transformations of the decade, choosing candidates based on the percentage
of revenue they receive from new, outside-the-core growth areas;
how successfully they repositioned their cores; and their overall
financial growth.

The common denominator for all of them, we found, was having a newly strengthened sense of purpose. Siemens, for example,
moved beyond a stated purpose of maximizing shareholder value
to an explicit mission of serving society. China's Tencent embraced
a mission of "improving the quality of human life through digital
innovation," investing heavily in new growth efforts ranging from
education and entertainment to autonomous vehicles, fintech,
and the industrial internet. In 2019, it refined its mission even more,
to a succinct "tech for social good."[29] Denmark's Ørsted transformed itself from a struggling natural gas business to a cutting-
edge wind energy company, increasing its net profits by some
$3 billion per year. The takeaway, our colleagues Scott Anthony,
Alasdair Trotter, and Evan Schwartz wrote in *Harvard Business
Review*, is that "in an era of relentless change, a company survives
and thrives based not on its size or performance at any given time
but on its ability to reposition itself to create a new future, and to
leverage a purpose-driven mission to that end."[30]

Peter Senge on the Importance of a Shared Vision

"A shared vision is not an idea . . . it is, rather, a force in people's hearts. . . . Few, if any forces in human affairs are as powerful. . . . While adaptive learning is possible without vision, generative learning occurs only when people are striving to accomplish something that matters deeply to them."[31]

We saw how deeply people care about a shared vision while talking to a group of Innosight analysts and associates about this chapter. Mark was reminiscing about the ways that Innosight's vision had evolved over the years, from our initial focus on technological disruption, to our drive to achieve a deeper understanding of business models and the roles of senior leaders, and finally our development of the visioning-to-strategy-to-action methods and processes we describe in this book.

"A lot of the younger people here don't know about that," one said. "Would you be willing to talk about it in an employee forum?" The next thing we knew, we had all opened our phones to our calendars, and the forum was scheduled. It turned out to be one of the liveliest and best attended we'd held in a long time. Despite all of Innosight's strategic pivots and shifts, we realized, we have remained steadfast in the mission and values we set for ourselves twenty years ago. In five to ten years, we hope the people in that room will still be tracking against that core identity, even as they evolve our company to its next phase of growth.

PART FOUR

BROADER IMPLICATIONS

When we shared early manuscript versions of this book with friends and colleagues, many of them cautioned us against overreaching. "If you want to fix the government or the military," one said, "you would have to write a completely different book." Others warned us that our approaches to climate change, healthcare, military procurement, and even the challenges of religious institutions could be received as grandiose or naïve (or both). "Stick to business," they said, "and leave those other issues to the experts."

But anyone who picks up a newspaper can see the experts are struggling. We don't presume we know more than they do, we don't. But we *do* believe there are better ways to frame our societal problems than the ones too many of those experts are using. Just as in business, sometimes it's not *what* you think but *how* you think that can make the critical difference.

Sustainability, relevance, and the quest for meaning are challenges leaders of organizations of every kind must grapple with in today's rapidly changing world. Future-back thinking can help.

———————

Chapter 8

MOVING BEYOND THE BUSINESS WORLD

Neither a wise man nor a brave man lies down
on the tracks of history to wait for the train
of the future to run over him.

—Dwight D. Eisenhower

The moonshot • Holding the wolf by the ear • Hillbilly armor • The 535-member board of directors • Universities vs. workforce accelerators • What do you want to be when you grow up? • Growth is not just about scale; value is not just about dollars

---

Think about the original moonshot: landing a man on the moon in less than a decade was a powerful, visionary challenge that galvanized the whole nation. As President John F. Kennedy declared in his May 25, 1961, speech, "We will do it not because it's easy, but because it's hard, because that goal will serve to organize and measure the best of our skills and talents." Having taken formal ownership of the initiative, President Kennedy (and Presidents Johnson and Nixon after him) ensured that it would have all the resources it needed. It was planned from its desired end-point backwards, with an escalating series of milestones. And Kennedy's challenge was backed up by an implementable strategy.

The already-existing Mercury program, created to send first animals and then men into suborbital and orbital flight, was followed by the Gemini program, whose maneuverable capsules carried two-man crews, stayed aloft for a week and more, and provided the astronauts with opportunities to walk in space and link up with other spacecraft. Finally, the Apollo program put all the pieces together, sending a three-man crew and a detachable lander all the way to the moon, at first to simply orbit it and return but ultimately to land two astronauts on its surface. As carefully planned and orchestrated as the original moonshot was, there were costly setbacks and lessons learned along the way, like the launch pad fire in 1967 that killed Gus Grissom, Ed White, and Roger Chaffee, and the oxygen explosion that nearly doomed Apollo 13.

Most beyond-business organizations have deep and inspiring missions, but, as with businesses, institutional structures and processes and their leaders' present-forward thinking can sometimes stand in the way of their goals. The government is prone to partisan gridlock; the military gets bogged down in its sometimes Byzantine procurement practices; while too many religious institutions and charities fall out of touch with the communities they intend to serve.

In this chapter, we will step outside of our usual purview as business strategists and suggest some of the benefits future-back thinking can bestow on noncommercial organizations—and the insights it can give into your own personal values. It would be presumptuous of us to advise government, charity, educational, and religious leaders to comport themselves more like business leaders. Different kinds of organizations have different needs, and as such, require different kinds of leaders. But we do believe the principles and methods we prescribe to business leaders can also help the leaders of other kinds of organizations address some of their most vexing challenges.

The US Government

For most of its history, the US government has worked as the Constitution intended it to. Because of the divisions between federal, state, and local authorities, and the many checks and balances between its legislative, executive, and judicial branches, the ship of state is cumbersome and hard to steer. Nonetheless, the national government has held together for most of the nearly 250 years it has existed. Along the way, it has undertaken projects of staggering scale and ambition, such as the transcontinental railroad, the Panama Canal, the interstate highway system, and the moonshot. Each was as visionary as the idea of America itself, conceived out of a bold vision of what could be, instead of what is.

But when it comes to wicked problems—quandaries so systemic, complex, and multifaceted they demand a national effort to solve them, but so politically and ideologically fraught people can't agree on how to define and frame them (never mind reach a consensus on a concerted program or strategy to overcome them)— our decentralized government can become paralyzed. The question of slavery, for example, was already dividing the country as the Constitution was being drafted. Both Washington and Jefferson feared the controversy would eventually spell the ruin of the Republic. "We have the wolf by the ear," Jefferson despaired, "and we can neither hold him, nor safely let him go."[1] It ultimately took four years of bloody warfare to settle the issue, and the nation is still struggling with its repercussions today.

Similarly, look at the impasse the United States is stuck in with healthcare. No one would have deliberately designed a healthcare system like ours, which spends more per capita than any of the other developed nations while delivering some of the worst outcomes (for just one example, the United States' disease burden, as measured by years lost to disease and disability, is 30 percent higher than in other wealthy countries).[2] The Affordable Care Act succeeded in its main goal of expanding access to care by applying patches to the system, but it was so fiercely attacked that many of its features were rolled back or excluded as it was implemented state by state. A host of thoughtful improvements have been proposed, but the heat of the debate is such that it is hopelessly distorted by dogma and bad faith. Partisans are either trapped in the present or the future, unable to envision an ideal system that could be and then work back from it to an actionable plan that can begin to move us toward it today.

When a government is "of the people," it is particularly vulnerable to the biases we described in chapter 1. Perhaps the starkest example of its inability to overcome the normalcy bias (our tendency to underrate the potential for catastrophe) is its failure to come to grips with the dilemma of global climate change. If its consequences will be half as catastrophic as an overwhelming consensus of scientists predict, climate change threatens not just America's coastal cities and farms but the very survival of the human species. Yet a large percentage of American voters and politicians have made their peace with it, much as they have lived with the threat of nuclear annihilation for the past half century and more. There are a host of reasons for this, some economic, some psychological, and some political. But the problem is clearly exacerbated by its present-forward framing.

While growing numbers are sounding the alarm, too many of America's leaders and citizens insist on framing the crisis and proposed efforts to forestall it from the perspective of the present. They begin by weighing the negative externalities that will be certain to occur in the near-term (higher gasoline taxes; setting your thermostat low in the winter and high in the summer; having your freedom of choice restricted in the marketplace; reversing the growth of carbon-dependent industries and possibly the nation's GDP) against the hypothetical future consequences of doing nothing. Those hypothetical consequences are: (1) distant in time; (2) not a 100 percent probability; (3) based on analyses of data that are not easy to understand and that don't always agree with each other; and (4) so devastating that the mind simply rebels.

Paying more to fill our SUVs' gas tanks is hard on our wallets, while the prospect of our grandchildren struggling to survive in a hellish dystopia sounds like something we'd see at the movies. Forcing fossil fuel producers to scale back their growth expectations and utilities to invest more than they want to in renewables is inviting pushback. It's easy to find excuses not to act—especially if you have a high tolerance for cognitive dissonance and are able to convince yourself that climate scientists, who have nothing to gain from their doomsaying, are in it for the money, while the carbon-dependent interests are disinterested.

On the other hand, we could ground our thinking in the future. If we begin by envisioning both the worst- and the best-case scenarios, objectively weighing the costs that would be incurred in each against the savings that would come from doing nothing, the opportunity costs our descendants will have to pay become much clearer, making it that much harder to keep kicking the can down the road. If the needed response is framed in a reverse chronology—to forestall the worst we have to accomplish d in twenty years, which is attainable if we do c by year ten, which we could easily accomplish if we managed to do just b in five years, which requires us to do a today—it would be much easier to get a handle on what is required. In fact, we've already made much progress that can be accelerated and leveraged (a shift to renewable energy and more sustainable systems for transportation and agriculture; the development of hybrid and fully electric vehicles; the potential for carbon dioxide removal technologies). It may be too late to avert all of the negative impacts of the crisis, but if we're ever going to summon up the will to act, we must start by believing what we do today will have real consequences for real people tomorrow. As the saying goes, if we can send a man to the moon, then why can't we *fill in the blank*? With a strong enough commitment to collaborative learning and problem solving, a sufficiently inspiring and actionable vision, and a leadership that is committed to change, we'd like to think we can.

The US Military

In 2003, the US Army launched an ambitious program called Future Combat Systems which, using Silicon Valley's spiral

Some Common Threads in Visionary, Future-back Projects

Governments are organizations too, and like businesses, they can be either future-facing or bound to the present. When you look at the largest-scale projects the United States has taken on in its history (putting a man on the moon; building the interstate highway system and the trans-continental railroad; developing the atom bomb; digging the Panama Canal), they all had certain features in common. First and foremost was a powerful vision. Each of them pro-posed to do what was seemingly impossible, drawing a stark line between what existed before and after. Beyond that, they leveraged:

- **A sense of urgency.** Putting a man on the moon had a clear deadline. The Manhattan Project was driven by the need to create a deployable weapon before the Germans did. The deadline scientists have set for averting the worst effects global warming is terrifyingly close.

- **Necessity.** The Panama Canal cut the journey from the Atlantic to the Pacific Ocean by 13,000 miles. Within the United States, frustrated travelers, businesses that needed to ship and receive raw materials and finished goods, and the military saw a national highway system as a vital ingredient of the country's infrastructure. In the summer of 1919, Dwight D. Eisenhower, then a 28-year-old lieuten-ant colonel, participated in a coast-to-coast journey with a 72-vehicle convoy organized by the Army's Motor Transport Corps that took 62 grueling days. As bad as the road conditions on the Lincoln Highway (the nation's nominal cross-country route) were on the early legs of their journey, when they reached Nebraska there were hardly any roads at all. Vehicles were mired in quicksand in the desert, and they struggled to traverse the mountains. In Utah and Nevada, the convoy's speed averaged five miles per hour and there were whole days when it covered as little as three. During the invasion and occupation of Germany, Eisenhower marveled at the multilane autobahn. "The old convoy had started me thinking about good, two-lane highways," he recalled. "But Germany made me see the wisdom of broader ribbons across the land."[3] As president, he signed the Interstate Highway Act into law.

- **Exploration.** Visionary projects are launched on the bleeding edge. The leaders of these great public works projects did things that hadn't been done before, opening up new territory (both figuratively and literally). Each began at times of change and transformation. Perhaps the United States undertakes fewer projects of this scale today because the proverbial edges of its map have been filled in (unlike China, which is building roads, railroad lines, and whole cities at a stupendous rate).

- **Competition.** Competition is a crucial catalyst for most visionary public works projects. In the case of the transcontinental railroad, the government literally pitted two companies against each other in a race to the center of the continent. The Manhattan Project was funded when it became known that Germany was working to develop its own atomic arsenal. The moonshot was a race with the USSR, which had gotten a head start in the conquest of space with the Sputnik.

- **Perseverance.** The Manhattan Project, the Apollo program, and the Panama Canal were all vastly expensive and suffered significant setbacks. Even so, national leaders found the funding and the wherewithal to push the projects to completion. The fact that things often don't go according to plan must be a part of the plan.

model for rapid technology development, was meant to create and deploy a visionary system-of-systems for ground combat revolving around robot tanks and drones. The target date for its rollout was 2025. In 2009, after some $20 billion had been expended to little effect, the program was unceremoniously shelved.

During those same six years, ironically, soldiers in Iraq had been reduced to retrofitting their Hummers and trucks with homemade, so-called hillbilly armor to protect themselves against improvised explosive devices, and carrying off-the-shelf walky-talkies into combat because the ones the army had issued didn't work. When a reporter asked then Defense Secretary Donald Rumsfeld why soldiers had been reduced to digging through landfills for scrap metal, he replied, "As you know, you go to war with the army you have, not the army you might want or wish to have at a later time." Rumsfeld also asked Lt. General R. Steven Whitcomb, the commander of army forces in the Persian Gulf, to address the question. "It's not a matter of money or desire," Whitcomb said. "It's a matter of the logistics of being able to produce it."[4]

We agree that the issue wasn't money or desire. As with businesses, resource allocation decisions at the highest levels play an enormous role in the success or failure of initiatives. Beyond that, we would argue that there was a failure of vision as well, specifically a failure to envision the military's future needs in the right ways and at the right time horizons—and to connect those visions to the present in actionable ways. Ever since the attacks of 9/11, the US military's primary challenge has been asymmetric warfare—combat with less well-armed, mostly nonstate actors, who are dispersed in remote areas. But its legacy structures and practices, and those of the massive contractors it depends on (Eisenhower's notorious military industrial complex) still incline it to hugely expensive projects that develop so slowly that they risk becoming redundant before they are deployed. The military's relationships with its contractors can be unhealthily synergistic; as often as not, it shapes its planning around their product cycles rather than the other way around.

We've argued that corporate planners tend to be too short-term in their thinking. In the case of the military, the opposite problem has sometimes prevailed. Its leaders need to think as deeply about the next five years as they do about the next twenty, and they need to build capabilities that will allow them to meet their logistic challenges in months instead of years or decades.

That said, the US military is very far from a poster child for non-future-back thinking. It is a learning organization par excellence, and it has significantly remade itself over the past two decades. The military engages in extensive scenario planning and has taught the business world much of what it knows about strategy. The US Army, for example, sets the standard for pre- and postmortems and after-action reports. Much to its credit, it has worked hard since 2009 to understand where the Future Combat Systems program went so wrong. And we would be remiss if we didn't acknowledge that the MRAP (mine-resistant ambush protected) program, which belatedly got off the ground in 2007, ultimately did deliver thousands of light armored vehicles to Iraq.

As thoughtful and well-developed as the military's long-term strategies are, it is less able than it should be to develop the visionary ideas that are urgently needed in the immediate present. Vision is about what the nature of warfare will be like tomorrow, and we are living in a world defined by volatility, uncertainty, complexity, and ambiguity (frequently shortened into the acronym VUCA). Yes, it's likely that another protracted ground war will occur someday, and the military must be prepared for it. Dauntingly complex and expensive aircraft, warships, cyber weapons, and even robot tanks and drones will be needed to fight it, and they take a long time to develop; satellites must be launched and maintained; new strategies must be developed and refined.

But it's even more likely our domestic power grid will be attacked by cyber terrorists, an American embassy in a far-off corner of the world will be fired on by an ad hoc group with a cache of stolen weapons, or a nation-state we hadn't particularly been paying attention to will invade a neighbor, destabilizing an entire region. The military must be able to anticipate things that have never happened before, swiftly develop new capabilities to respond to or preempt them, and at the same time, *stop* doing things that it no longer needs to do.

Some of the military's lack of agility stems from sheer size. It has 1.2 million men and women in uniform, and they're led by 1,000 flag officers. Each of the armed services has its own bureaucracy, which is set in its present-forward ways of thinking and doing, and each is answerable to the civilian government, which is even bigger and more bureaucratic. Structure and civilian resource allocation decisions shape its operational and strategic thinking at every level. Meanwhile, its civilian leaders change with every new administration, and its senior officers are constantly being rotated into new commands. The problem with leadership continuity in businesses we addressed in chapter 7 is even more acute in the military. "I report to a 535-member board of directors," a general once told Mark (meaning the House of Representatives and the US Senate). "The secretary of defense changes between and within administrations, and I'm only in this position for a few years, until they rotate me out to another assignment. Even if I do make some headway, my successors have to reinvent the wheel."

To develop a real actionable vision about what the nature of threats like cyber warfare will be in three to five years, military and civilian leaders from the top to the bottom of the command structure must shift more of their thinking to the right side of the leadership framework and spend more time in an explore, envision, and discover mode. When new leaders come in, they need to continue those efforts and not simply reset things to their default positions on the left.

In 2018, the US Army announced the formation of a new Army Futures Command (AFC) to modernize its weaponry, organization, training, and acquisition processes. One of its goals is to reduce the time it takes to define its technical requirements for acquisitions from sixty to twelve months. With its emphasis on outside partnerships and rapid prototyping so new initiatives can "fail early and cheaply, and then increase learning,"[5] it is clearly on the right path. But while twelve months is a lot shorter than sixty months, it's still a long time when people are being killed. The AFC's chief challenge, we suspect, will be to ensure that it not become as captive to its newer-and-better structures and processes as its predecessors were to their old ones—that it develops and retains the capacity to vision and revision so it can fight the wars of the future with the army that it both wants and needs to have.

Higher Education

American higher education faces a number of challenges that will likely combine and tip in the next decade, among them a demographic shift that will reduce the number of traditional college-aged students (starting around 2025, the number of high school graduates is projected to decline precipitously, by as much as 20 percent in some regions). A perfect storm is brewing, as the public clamors for more affordable or even free college educations at the same time that state and national governments radically reduce the funding they supply to support public education. Given the unsustainably high levels four-year-school tuitions have reached already—they have tripled over the past three decades, far out-pacing inflation, wage growth, and the means of many middle-class families to pay them or manage the debt they must incur to do so—most colleges will not be able to fill their growth gaps by raising their tuitions even higher.

Meanwhile, the continuing rise of new entrants through online education is challenging the traditional model for college education. Schools will likely place a greater emphasis on job training and certificate programs than they do today, reaching out to include more adult learners in their classrooms (virtual and bricks-and-mortar). To maintain their revenue streams, many will develop or expand partnerships with governments and corporations to provide targeted research and specialized training. Others will likely undertake dual transformations, optimizing their cores by streamlining their cost structures, centralizing their administrations and removing layers from them, eliminating duplication across schools and departments, culling their least successful programs, and making deeper investments in the ones with the most potential. Further, they will protect and build their endowments with better investment strategies, and work to improve their academic brands.

Some of this is already happening. The workforce accelerator Trilogy Education, a for-profit enterprise that provides training, professional certification, and job placement assistance to students, may be a harbinger of what's to come. So is Southern New Hampshire University, which has vastly expanded its profile and its footprint by building its College of Online & Continuing Education, which grew from 8,000 students in 2001 to 80,000 today.

Still, the likeliest outcome in the nearer-term is disruption, with many small liberal arts schools and underperforming state and community colleges with low completion rates being forced to merge to create economies of scale, change beyond recognition, or close their doors. A few years ago, Clay Christensen predicted that as many as half of American universities will go bankrupt within the next decade or so—a percentage that has been widely challenged, but as with climate change, even the best-case scenarios are troubling.[6]

How can a future-back framework help the leaders of colleges and universities make better choices? As the leaders of Australia's Deakin University did, looking out ten years and more forces them to think harder about the new environment they must survive in, the jobs to be done of their future students, and the implications for their current practices. Many will realize that business as usual is no longer sustainable. For them, developing a viable future state portfolio is an existential imperative.

More importantly still, it will force them to revisit their vision and values and ask themselves some gut-wrenching questions. Can the liberal arts curriculum survive? Will students still read the classics and study history, ancient languages, comparative religion, and philosophy, or will all of that fall by the wayside as colleges turn their focus to the STEM disciplines (science, technology, engineering, and mathematics), business, and other practical areas that can justify their cost by qualifying students for high-paying jobs? Will universities become extensions of corporate research and development and Human Resources—or turn into venture capital incubators, real estate developers, sports franchises, and business consultancies? How can they cut costs while still delivering quality educations to as many students as possible? In chapter 3, we said leaders should use their deepest aspiration as their touchstones. Building a future state portfolio, we said, gives you the opportunity to design the ideal organization of the future, irrespective of what it is today. Taking that to heart may mean making the choice to become smaller but more effective, to do fewer things better.

Every leader will approach these questions in different ways; our task is not to prescribe the solutions but to provide the ways of thinking that will allow the best answers to come to the surface. Simply taking the future seriously, acknowledging the urgency of the crisis and the need to change in fundamental ways to meet is a big step forward.

Like America's healthcare system, our higher education system serves a vital and growing need. At its best, it is the envy of the world. But it's also safe to say no one would have deliberately designed as inefficient, costly, and unsustainable a model for it as we have now. There are as many potential strategies to fix our system for higher education and make it more sustainable as there are schools and students.

Churches, Charities, and Activist Organizations

When we told a colleague about this book, she remarked rather wistfully about how eager children are to engage with the future.

Beguiled by the wonders of space travel, flying cars, and other miraculous advances, they talk endlessly about what they want to be when they grow up. But as they get older, their imaginations become less vivid and their view of the possible more constrained. "Envisioning in the way that you describe," she said, "Is about reawakening the most creative parts of ourselves. Executives should regard the time they set aside for thinking about the future as an almost sacred obligation, like going to church."

In principle, churches and other religious institutions are built upon a foundation of vision, but when you look into their back offices, where the humdrum work of temporal administration is carried out, most look and feel much like any other present-forward organization—sometimes so much so that it interferes with their ability to fulfill their customers' spiritual jobs to be done. Though it might sound like bringing coals to Newcastle, future-back thinking can also help the leaders of religious institutions reconnect with their loftiest purposes.

Most of the people who administer religious institutions are people of deep faith and conviction. But they tend to spend more of their time on the left side of the leadership framework than is good for either them or the faith communities they work so hard to serve. As interested as they are in eternity, they rarely look ahead more than a few years when they are making their resource allocation decisions. It's not that the present-forward, operate-and-execute activities they prioritize aren't important. Their human and material resources are limited and therefore must be apportioned wisely. Budgets need to be drawn up and closely adhered to; religious school curricula proposed, approved, and developed. Professional staffs need to be hired and trained; volunteers coordinated; real estate bought and sold.

But to borrow a phrase, man does not live by bread alone. Like the military, religious institutions must contend with all of our VUCA challenges, from cyber threats and terrorism, to the material and spiritual repercussions of climate change and income inequality. Gender roles, indeed gender itself, is being questioned. Genetic engineering, artificial intelligence, and robotics are changing our conception of what it means to be human—and the singularity, the moment when computers become smarter than people, is rapidly approaching. To stay relevant to its members, religious leaders must overcome the tyranny of the urgent, step off the present-forward treadmill of project reviews and financial projections, and move to the right side of the leadership framework, asking themselves such hard questions as:

- What must we do and what must we stop doing to ensure that we attract, serve, and retain all the members of our communities—and new adherents as well?

- As we expand our global footprint, how do we ensure that we form enduring relationships with our new members?

- Are younger members, women, and gay people leaving our faith because they perceive its message and its programming as hostile or retrograde? Doctrine permitting, what can we do to change that?

- Are we using the right metrics to measure our successes and failures? How do we keep them simple and focused?

- What are the impediments to change? Are we putting stumbling blocks in our own path?

This goes way beyond mere messaging. In spiritual as in secular organizations, resource allocation speaks louder than words. Future-back thinking can help religious leaders decide which activities should be standardized and centralized to drive uniformity and consistency, and which diversified and decentralized so local leaders can customize to better meet their communities' particular needs. It can help them take the long-view when they consider who and what gets more, and who and what gets less, and how they can help those who will get less to adjust. Putting vision first will remind them that their goal is to ensure the continuing relevance and sustainability of their organization, not to simply maintain and preserve it as it is.

Charities, nonprofits, and activist groups can similarly become prisoners of their structures and short-term interests, rather than emissaries of the transcendent missions and goals they came into being to serve. The need to be sustainable can devolve into a push to grow for the sake of growth, while the desire to stay true to one's founding values can lapse into a kind of cultish extremism. The competition for scarce resources like donations and talent can cause them to be overly secretive and hence heedless of the consequences for the future—for example, hiding their failures rather than publishing them and sharing them in public forums so that other organizations that are working the same territory can learn from them. It can lead them to protect a leader who has misused his or her position because they excel at fundraising or are inextricably identified with their brand. And like so many for-profit organizations, nonprofits can become stuck in the past, retaining practices and programs long after they have become obsolete. As Peter Drucker wrote, "Sloughing off yesterday is particularly important these days for the non-business public service institution. It is all but impossible for most of them to accept that success always means organizing for the abandonment of what has already been achieved. In turbulent times, an enterprise needs to be able both to outride sudden hard blows and to avail itself of sudden unexpected opportunities."[7]

> The discipline of future-back thinking compels leaders to ask hard questions about both their future and their present—and reminds them of their ultimate purpose.

Future-back Yourself

Future-back thinking and strategy development are key competencies for leaders of long-established organizations. But can you use them to help you fulfill your personal goals? You can, up to a point, but perhaps not in the way that you think.

As innovative and thoughtful as many leadership development programs are, their records are spotty when it comes to identifying the leaders who are ready for advancement to the very highest levels. Sadly, the single biggest cause of director and higher terminations are ill-starred promotions of the sort that inspired Laurence J. Peter to identify what we now call the Peter Principle: "In a hierarchy every employee tends to rise to his level of incompetence."[8] Taking a future-back approach to career development (designing high-promise executives' career tracks backwards, starting from their intended destinations) could help reduce some of that churn for the people you oversee and for yourself. Having a clear idea of your intended destination (future-back planning) allows you to make better choices as opportunities present themselves (emergent planning).

Many career choices fall squarely under the heading of common sense. *Know your strengths and leverage them; be cognizant of your weaknesses and be sure to compensate for them. Don't stay in a job that requires you to work against the grain of your values.* But we would be disingenuous if we said that it's as easy to create an actionable vision for yourself as it is for an organization, because, first, it's not easy for organizations either; and second, because the future-back strategies organizations pursue are almost always directed toward goals that can ultimately be captured by financial or other kinds of quantitative metrics.

Your long-term goals as an individual are much harder to quantify, because success will mean different things to you at different times in your life. Making money and achieving power are important to many people, but at the end of the day, both are means to ends. As we are far from the first to observe, when rich and powerful people are on their deathbeds, they tend to want the same things that everyone else does—the presence of a loving touch, the assurance that their lives added up to something worthwhile, that they made a difference in the world.

Your personal visions and values and your professional aspirations may seem to run on different tracks, but sometimes, especially at those crucible moments that define a leader, they can come together decisively. In 1982, when someone laced Johnson & Johnson's Tylenol brand capsules with cyanide, killing seven people, James Burke, J&J's CEO at the time, swiftly recalled every Tylenol product from store shelves nationwide and destroyed them. That prompt and transparent response helped J&J regain its customers' trust when it re-released Tylenol in tamperproof packaging a few months later—and allowed it to recapture all of the market share it had lost within a year. Burke gave credit to the famous credo Robert Wood Johnson II, the son of one of J&J's founders, wrote when he took the company public in 1943. The credo formalizes J&J's responsibilities to its customers, its employees, the public at large, the planet, the future, and only last and as a matter of course, its shareholders ("when we operate according to these principles, the stockholders should realize a fair return").[9] "The credo," Burke said, "made it very clear at that point exactly what we were all about. It gave me the ammunition I needed to persuade shareholders and others to spend the $100 million on the recall."[10] Of course, other companies that have handled crises less honorably or adeptly have also published value statements just as high-minded as J&J's—and J&J itself has come in for its own share of criticism. When push comes to shove, what really makes the difference is the character and courage of individual leaders.

For all of our emphasis on strategy in other realms, we recognize that serendipity plays a huge part in what a lot of very successful people end up doing with their lives. Most successful romantic partnerships begin by happenstance, and few of us have the opportunity to future-back the trajectories of our children's lives, as much as we may wish we could. Where visioning and future-back thinking become truly important for individuals is when the goal is not to predict or reverse-engineer one's desired future but to understand what those desires really are. You must ask yourself hard, open-ended questions, and pay as much attention to your intuitions and your feelings as you do to your present-forward logic. *What do I truly want? What do I truly value? What will be meaningful to me in ten or twenty years? Are the choices I am making compatible with those things?*

Growth is not just about scale; value is not only about dollars. As the economist John Maynard Keynes wryly put it, "In the long run, we are all dead."[11] But in the time we have in this world, there is much that we can do to grow our characters while working to ensure a better, more-sustainable future for the generations to come. At the end of the day, the same is true for organizations, no matter what their size, sector, or ecosystem may be. In the time they have, all of them must change, regenerate, and grow in capability and focus.

A VISION FOR TWENTY-FIRST-CENTURY MANAGEMENT

At its most basic level, stewardship is acting upon the understanding that leadership is a temporary role which is outlasted by the lifespan of an organization.

—Bekele Geleta

Founder/leaders of startups enjoy the unique advantage of being able to concentrate all of their own, their teams', and their organizations' capabilities and efforts toward one great goal, which is to bring a singular vision into the world and then scale it. Google, Amazon, Netflix, and Facebook are young enough that their founders are still on the scene, so they are less wedded to their current ways of doing things, more willing to embrace new ideas, and focused on a much more distant time horizon than most leaders of long-established companies. Jeff Bezos, a future-back thinker if there ever was one, envisioned Amazon as an engine of continuous growth and transformation from its inception. The headline on his first shareholder letter was "It's All About the Long Term."[1] "As a company," he told *Wired* in 2011, "we are culturally pioneers, and we like to disrupt even our own business. If everything you do needs to work on a three-year time horizon, then you're competing against a lot of people. But if you're willing to invest on a seven-year time horizon, you're now competing against a fraction of those people, because very few companies are willing to do that. Just by lengthening the time horizon, you can engage in endeavors that you could never otherwise pursue. At Amazon . . . we're willing to plant seeds, let them grow—and we're very stubborn. We say we're stubborn on vision and flexible on details."[2]

Reed Hastings had such a clear vision of what Netflix could become, and such a well-developed strategy to get there, that he anticipated its shift from DVD rentals to streaming from the outset, before the technology had been fully developed. It's all laid out in the S-1 (the SEC filing that companies that are about to go public must make) that Netflix released in 2002: "VOD [Video on Demand] is now widely deployed in most major hotels, and has early deployments in many major cable systems. . . . We believe that our strategy of developing a large and growing subscriber base and our ability to personalize our library to each subscriber by leveraging our extensive database of user preferences positions us favorably to provide digital distribution of filmed entertainment as that market develops."[3]

Google's S-1, released two years after Netflix's, opened with a letter to investors from its cofounder Larry Page, in which he declared, "As a private company, we have concentrated on the long term, and this has served us well. As a public company," he asserted, "we will do the same."

> In our opinion, outside pressures too often tempt companies to sacrifice long-term opportunities to meet quarterly market expectations. . . . If opportunities arise that might cause us to sacrifice short-term results but are in the best long-term interest of our shareholders, we will take those opportunities. We will have the fortitude to do this. . . . We will not shy away from high-risk, high-reward projects because of short-term earnings pressure. Some of our past

bets have gone extraordinarily well, and others have not. Because we recognize the pursuit of such projects as the key to our long-term success, we will continue to seek them out. For example, we would fund projects that have a 10% chance of earning a billion dollars over the long term. Do not be surprised if we place smaller bets in areas that seem very speculative or even strange.[4]

Leaders of long-established organizations of scale face a different challenge, which is to both optimize the products and business models that make up their cores while simultaneously ensuring that pipelines of new products and business models are in development to supplement or replace them over time. This requires them to constantly toggle back and forth between present-forward and future-back thinking. Because of the tyranny of the urgent, their innate cognitive biases, the financial metrics and incentives that put a premium on short-term results, and budgeting and strategic development processes that formalize the present-forward fallacy, it's not surprising so many of them do much less toggling than they should.

Wouldn't it be something if the same kinds of aspirations that are written into future-facing S-1s also became the stuff of the annual reports of established enterprises? Having a ten-year horizon and a future-back perspective would make so much possible.

When all is said and done, this has been a book about how to manage time. Not time management in the sense most people think of it, optimizing your daily calendar to ensure that you are squeezing as much productivity as you can out of every hour, but how you orient yourself and your business to the past, present, and future.

> Having a clear vision of your intended future allows you to anticipate and grasp opportunities for breakthrough growth—and to stop doing the things that are becoming irrelevant.

No, you don't have a crystal ball; nobody does. But you know a lot more than you think you do about the ways things are trending, and if you work as a team with your peers, combining and recombining your insights, you can learn much more. As the futurist Bob Johansen puts it, the idea is to hone in on what you know will be different while reducing your overconfidence in business-as-usual. "The future will reward clarity," he says, "but punish certainty."[5]

It is difficult, but not impossible, for big, incumbent organizations to initiate and sustain the efforts that are required to drive growth within the core while simultaneously generating breakthrough growth outside it. Moreover, that is something any good leader can do; you don't have to be a larger-than-life superhero like Steve Jobs or Jeff Bezos to be a practical visionary.

Without vision, there is only the push of the short term and no pull of the future. With it, you can not only anticipate the future but help to create it. For all the far-seeing books that futurists write, the white papers about coming trends that think tanks and academic institutions churn out, and the hard work that strategists and long-term investors do to crack the code of the future, none that we know of provide what we have in these pages: a theoretical foundation for a different way of thinking and a step-by-step process that applies it to build and maintain the bridges that connect your organization's tomorrow to its today.

Evolve or Die

"Evolve or die" is a cliché, and not a particularly pretty one, but it reflects a stark truth. Around the time we started writing this book, the business press was buzzing about a meeting at Amazon's Seattle headquarters. An employee had asked Jeff Bezos what he thought about the recent bankruptcy of Sears, which has been dubbed the original Amazon ("to understand Amazon," Derek Thompson wrote in *The Atlantic* a few years ago, "its evolution, its strategy, and perhaps its future—look to Sears").[6] Bezos didn't miss a beat. "Amazon is not too big to fail," he reportedly replied. "In fact, I predict one day Amazon *will* fail. Amazon will go bankrupt."[7]

He is right, of course. No matter how far-seeing you may be, no matter how enterprising, death comes for everyone; it's just a matter of time. And big organizations are shorter-lived than they have ever been. In 1958, the average tenure of a company on the S&P 500 was thirty-three years. It dropped to twenty-four years as of 2016 and it is projected to shrink to twelve by 2027. At that churn rate, half of the companies on the S&P 500 will be replaced in the next decade.[8] Some of them will be acquired or merged, some might be taken private, but many of them will have ceased to grow and shrunk below the minimum level of capitalization required to be listed on the benchmark index. Some will disappear altogether. That's a hard pill to swallow if you're a leader of one of these giants, not just because it's painful to contemplate but because it seems so unreal.

The stark certainty of our eventual extinction and, at the same time, our inability to imagine a world without us, is much more than a business problem—it is the essence of the human condition. Still, it's ironic that Bezos would have sounded as fatalistic about Amazon's ultimate fate as he did, because Amazon is not a person but an organization, and Bezos has done as much as any business leader ever has to ensure that the company he founded retains the questing mentality of an entrepreneurial startup, even as it has scaled into one of the biggest and most successful enterprises in the world. "Day 2 is stasis," he declared in one of his most quoted annual shareholder letters. "Followed by irrelevance. Followed by excruciating, painful decline. Followed by death. And *that* is why it is *always* Day 1."[9]

Unlike human beings, whose lifespans have fairly set ceilings, well-run, adaptable organizations can and do regenerate themselves. Waning business units can be replaced with newer and more vital ones; new technologies can be embraced and leveraged for renewed growth. Even a fallen giant like GE may turn itself around; for the sake of its many stakeholders, we hope it does.

To stave off day 2 for as long as possible, an enterprise can never be content to be; only to become. Its leaders must have the resilience and the willingness to take risks and learn from them—and to do so continually, forever managing for the present while learning and leading toward a better future.

As Charles Handy wrote all the way back in 1989, in his then much-talked about book *The Age of Unreason*, it is no use "delegating the [big] questions . . . to some groups of scenario planners, corporate planners, or even outside consultants. If the key executives feel no ownership of the questions and the theories, they will not want to take the risk of testing them. . . . Top executives themselves have to be the ones who ask the questions, seek out the ideas . . . test the best of them and then, deliberately, take time out to reflect on the results."[10] If it's now widely understood that the teams that are entrusted with strategy-making, design, and new product development must take a longer view and think more creatively, the biggest lesson that should have come out of the vogue for the learning organization has somehow been lost—that leaders and leadership teams themselves must clear time from their schedules and make room in their mental bandwidth for questioning and exploring, visioning and discovering.

In the future, the organizations that lead and succeed will be the ones that never stop learning.

We hope this book will reignite a passion for questioning and learning among the leaders of organizations of all kinds. We have a higher hope too, which is that in thinking hard about what they *could* be, leaders will also converge on an idea of what they *should* be. We have more than a professional interest in the future. We are also parents, and as such, we have skin in the game.

Short-term thinking can be selfish and dangerous, and in real ways an abdication of a profound responsibility. In December of 2018, Seth Klarman, the CEO and portfolio manager of the Baupost Group, a hedge fund with $27 billion in assets, delivered a speech at Harvard Business School in which he underlined its corrosive effects.

"One of society's most vexing problems," he declared, "is the relentlessly short-term orientation that manifests itself in investing, in business decision making, and in our politics. . . . A big part of leadership is deciding, and good decision-making benefits from intelligence, thoughtful deliberation, and experience, but also as I hope you agree, from sound values. Choosing what to maximize, how, and over what time frame, is an expression of those values."[11]

So much of the literature about business leadership frames it in a military context. Leaders are cast as generals whose role is to enable a team or an organization to carry out a mission with victory as its ultimate goal—defeating the enemy (the competition) and seizing the spoils (profits). We are not starry-eyed idealists; we are capitalists, of course. We appreciate the importance of winning in the marketplace and we work hard to help our clients do so. But we also believe that sound leadership, even of a competitive, for-profit organization, can be constructive and generative.

You must be something of a visionary to lead a great organization—but you must also be a steward of its legacy, of the people who depend on you for their livelihoods, and of society and the whole planet, all of whom need you to make the right choices. Future-back thinking and processes don't reveal a future that has always been predestined—they give you the opportunity and the means to shape it and own it.

"Good stewardship," notes Bekele Geleta, the former director general of the Red Cross, "allows any organization to continually develop and adjust to an ever-changing world. At its most basic level, stewardship is acting upon the understanding that leadership is a temporary role which is outlasted by the lifespan of an organization. A leader is performing the act of stewardship whenever he or she is actively preparing for an organization's future vitality."[12]

Most of the management doctrine we live by today was created more than a century ago to ensure efficiency and repeatability. The organization was seen as a great bureaucratic machine that melded people's individual efforts into vast, impersonal processes. Top executives were expected to be dispassionate numbers crunchers who rendered decisions based solely on financial metrics. Productivity matters as much as it ever has, but as we look out into the twenty-first century, when, ironically, more of the work of production and even routine administration really will be carried out by robots, the greatest challenge big organizations face will not be solved by algorithms but (as they have always been) by the wise men and women who look ahead and make the best choices.

As we see it, future-back thinking is not just a tool to help leaders gain the knowledge, the foresight, and the actionable ideas that enable breakthrough growth but a way of seeing and being in the world.

In the fifth century BCE, the philosopher Heraclitus wrote that "there is nothing permanent except change." As the world spins faster and faster and the pace of disruption accelerates, we believe that future-back thinking, leadership, and management will become—that they *must* become—the basis for a continuous strategic management system, and as such, the new normal. With what you've learned in this book, we hope that you will help pioneer and advance this new discipline, leading not just your organizations but all of us to a more prosperous, equitable, and sustainable way of life.

Notes

A Tribute to a True Visionary

1. "Business Roundtable Redefines the Purpose of a Corporation to Promote 'An Economy that Serves All Americans,'" Business Roundtable (website), August 19, 2019, https://www.businessroundtable.org/business -roundtable-redefines-the-purpose-of-a-corporation-to-promote-an -economy-that-serves-all-americans.

Introduction

1. Joseph Schumpeter (1883–1950). "The opening up of new markets, foreign or domestic, and the organizational development from the craft shop to such concerns as U.S. Steel illustrate the same process of industrial mutation . . . that incessantly revolutionizes the economic structure from within, incessantly destroying the old one incessantly creating a new one. This process of Creative Destruction is the essential fact about capitalism." Schumpeter, *Capitalism, Socialism, and Democracy* (New York: Harper Perennial Modern Thought, 2008), 83.

2. Proprietary Survey conducted by Innosight, summer 2019 (unpublished).

3. Clayton M. Christensen, *The Innovator's Dilemma: When New Technologies Cause Great Firms to Fail* (Boston: Harvard Business Review Press, 2016).

4. Wendell Weeks, from the transcript of Innosight's CEO Summit, Boston, MA, August 8, 2019.

5. Christensen, *Innovator's Dilemma*, 13.

Chapter 1

1. Herbert A. Simon, *Administrative Behavior* (New York: Macmillan, 1997), 119.

2. Daniel Gilbert, "If Only Gay Sex Caused Global Warming," *LA Times*, July 2, 2006, https://www.latimes.com/archives/la-xpm-2006-jul-02-op -gilbert2-story.html.

3. Clayton Christensen, *The Innovator's Dilemma* (Boston: Harvard Business Review Press, 2016).

4. A. G. Lafley, telephone interview with the authors, August 16, 2019.

5. Clayton Christensen and Derek van Bever, "The Capitalist's Dilemma," *Harvard Business Review*, June 2014, 60–68.

6. Roger L. Martin, "The Age of Customer Capitalism," *Harvard Business Review*, January–February 2010, 59–65.

7. Scott Cook, telephone interview with the authors, September 6, 2019.

8. Charles E. Hummel, *Tyranny of the Urgent* (Downers Grove, IL: InterVarsity Press, 1994).

9. Michael E. Porter and Nitin Nohria, "How CEOs Manage Time," *Harvard Business Review*, July–August 2018, 42–51.

10. Sandi Peterson, telephone interview with the authors, April 17, 2019.

11. Cook, telephone interview.

12. Cook, telephone interview.

13. Roger Martin, from the transcript of Innosight's CEO Summit, Lexington, MA, 2015.

Chapter 2

1. Steve Jobs, "You've Got to Find What You Love," *Stanford News*, June 14, 2005, https://news.stanford.edu/2005/06/14/jobs-061505/.

2. Walter Isaacson, *Steve Jobs* (New York: Simon & Schuster, 2011), 532.

3. See, for example, Tim Brown, *Change by Design: How Design Thinking Transforms Organizations and Inspires Innovation* (New York: HarperBusiness, 2009); Roger Martin, *The Design of Business: Why Design Thinking Is the Next Competitive Advantage* (Boston: Harvard Business School Publishing, 2009).

4. See also Mark W. Johnson and Josh Suskewicz, "How to Jump-Start the Clean Tech Economy," *Harvard Business Review*, November 2009, 52–63.

5. Thomas P. Hughes, "The Electrification of America: The System Builders," *Journal of Technology and Culture* 20, no. 1 (January 1979), quoted in Johnson and Suskewicz, "How to Jump-Start the Clean Tech Economy."

6. Peter F. Drucker, "The Theory of the Business," *Harvard Business Review*, September–October 1994.

7. Wendell Potter, "Analysis: The End of Health Insurance as We Know It?," The Center for Public Integrity, March 5, 2012, https://publicintegrity.org/health/analysis-the-end-of-health-insurance-as-we-know-it/.

8. "Who We Are," Aetna, accessed November 8, 2019, https://www.aetnastory.com/who-we-are.html.

9. Satya Nadella, *Hit Refresh: The Quest to Rediscover Microsoft's Soul and Imagine a Better Future for Everyone* (New York: HarperBusiness, 2016), 15.

10. Though numerous versions of the quote have been attributed to Edison, the most accurate, according to a fascinating article in the online Quote Investigator (https://quoteinvestigator.com/2012/04/10/rich-burn-candles/), appeared in the *New York Herald* on January 4, 1880: "'After the

electric light goes into general use,' said he, 'none but the extravagant will burn tallow candles.'"

11. *Macmillan Dictionary* Online, s.v. "vision," accessed November 7, 2019, https://www.macmillandictionary.com/dictionary/american /vision.

12. Nadella, *Hit Refresh*, 92.

13. Carol Dweck, *Mindset: The New Psychology of Success* (New York: Random House, 2006), 46–47.

14. Warren Bennis, *On Becoming a Leader* (New York: BasicBooks, 2009), 197.

15. Quote shared by David Garvin with Mark Johnson, source and date unknown.

16. Bernard C. Kummerli, Scott D. Anthony, and Markus Messerer, "Unite Your Senior Team," *Harvard Business Review*, November 2018, 60–69.

17. Peter Drucker, *Managing for Results* (New York: HarperCollins, 1986), 87–88.

18. Wendell Weeks, from the transcript of Innosight's CEO Summit, Boston, MA, August 8, 2019.

19. Rita Gunther McGrath and Ian MacMillan, "Discovery-Driven Planning," *Harvard Business Review*, July–August 1995, 44–54.

20. Clay Christensen, *The Innovator's Solution: Creating and Sustaining Successful Growth* (Boston: Harvard Business School Press, 2003), 78.

21. Clay Christensen, Karen Dillon, Taddy Hall, and David S. Duncan, *Competing against Luck: The Story of Innovation and Customer Choice* (New York: HarperBusiness, 2016), 29.

Part Two

1. Innosight has a long-standing relationship with William Hait. The authors carried out a formal telephone interview with him on April 19, 2019.

2. Hait, telephone interview.

Chapter 3

1. *Cyberpunk*, directed by Marianne Trench (Intercon Production, 1990).

2. Anthony R. Tersigni, "Healthcare, Disrupt Thyself: How Ascension Makes Changes Today to Thrive Tomorrow," *Journal of Healthcare Management* 63, no. 6 (November–December 2018): 370–373.

3. "Ascension Health formed Ascension in 2012 to further its Mission of serving all persons, especially those living in poverty and who are struggling the most, and to deliver compassionate, personalized care and lead healthcare transformation in the United States." Ascension, "About

Us—History," accessed December 3, 2019, https://ascension.org/about
/history.

4. Proprietary and confidential Janssen strategy document, 2016.

Chapter 4

1. Scott D. Anthony, Clark G. Gilbert, and Mark W. Johnson, *Dual Transformation: How to Reposition Today's Business while Creating the Future*
(Boston: Harvard Business Review Press, 2017).

2. A. G. Lafley, telephone interview with the authors, August 16, 2019.

Chapter 5

1. David Jacquemont, Dana Maor, and Angelika Reich, "How to Beat
the Transformation Odds," McKinsey & Company, April 2015, https://www
.mckinsey.com/business-functions/organization/our-insights/how-to
-beat-the-transformation-odds

2. Ben Wiegand, telephone interview with the authors, June 18, 2019.

3. Leigh Buchanan, "The CEO's Most Important Job, According to
Panera's Ron Shaich," *Inc. Magazine*, July–August, 2014, https://www.inc
.com/magazine/201407/leigh-buchanan/a-ceos-most-important-job
-according-to-paneras-ron-shaich.html.

4. A. G. Lafley, telephone interview with the authors, August 16, 2019.

5. Steve Nordlund, from the transcript of Innosight's CEO Summit,
Boston, MA, August 8, 2019.

6. Mark Johnson, *Reinvent Your Business Model: How to Seize the White
Space for Transformative Growth* (Boston: Harvard Business Review Press,
2018), 152–166.

7. Wiegand, telephone interview.

8. Roy Davis, personal conversation with Josh Suskewicz, date
unknown.

9. Logan Jones, from the transcript of Innosight's CEO Summit, Boston,
MA, August 8, 2019.

10. Rita Gunther McGrath and Ian MacMillan, "Discovery-Driven Planning," *Harvard Business Review*, July–August 1995,: 44–54; Scott D. Anthony,
The First Mile (Boston: Harvard Business School Press, 2014).

11. Clark Gilbert, Mark Johnson, and Scott D. Anthony, *Dual Transformation* (Boston: Harvard Business Review Publishing, 2017).

12. Johnson, *Reinvent Your Business Model*.

13. William Hait, telephone interview with the authors, April 19,
2019.

14. Avrum Spira, telephone interview with the authors, August 21,
2019.

15. Hait, telephone interview.

Chapter 6

1. Jeffrey Bezos, "2005 Annual Shareholder Letter," Amazon, accessed October 18, 2019, https://ir.aboutamazon.com/static-files/2eb4e2f3-fcaa -4bbe-8347-9900c904ab4f.

2. Charles A. O'Reilly III and Michael L. Tushman, "The Ambidextrous Organization," *Harvard Business Review*, April 2004, 74–81.

3. See, for example, Gary Hamel and Bill Breen, *The Future of Management* (Boston: Harvard Business School Press, 2007).

4. Udit Batra, interview with the authors, Burlington, MA, September 24, 2018.

5. *Arthurian Chronicles Represented by Wace and Layamon* (New York: E. P. Dutton, 1921), 55.

6. Alice M. Cahill and Laura Quinn, "Are You Getting the Best out of Your Executive Team?," Center for Creative Leadership, accessed October 18, 2018, https://www.ccl.org/articles/white-papers/getting-best-executive-team/.

7. Mike Leavitt, telephone interview with the authors, June 25, 2018.

8. Jim Collins, *Good to Great: Why Some Companies Make the Leap . . . and Others Don't* (New York: HarperCollins, 2001), 13.

9. David Henshall, interview with the authors, Fort Lauderdale, FL, June 25, 2018.

10. Terry Crimmins, interview with the authors, Nashua, NH, July 25, 2018.

11. Bob Rivers, interview with the authors, Boston, July 3, 2018.

12. Chris Chadwick, telephone interview with the authors, September 18, 2018.

13. Herminia Ibarra, *Act Like a Leader, Think Like a Leader* (Boston: Harvard Business Review Press, 2015), 2.

14. Rivers, interview.

15. Sandi Peterson, telephone interview with the authors, April 17, 2019.

16. Rich Bane, telephone interview with authors, May 6, 2019.

17. Peterson, telephone interview.

18. Chadwick, telephone interview.

Chapter 7

1. Admiral James Stavridis, interview with the authors, Cambridge, MA, May 15, 2018.

2. World Without Disease Strategic Narrative (proprietary and confidential).

3. A. G. Lafley, telephone interview with authors, August 16, 2019.

4. Jim Collins, *Good to Great* (New York: HarperBusiness, 2001), 45–46.

5. Jack Dorsey, from the transcript of Innosight's CEO Summit, Boston, MA, August 8, 2019.

6. Lafley, telephone interview.

7. Scott Cook, telephone interview with the authors, September 9, 2019.

8. Cook, telephone interview.

9. Sandi Peterson, telephone interview with the authors, April 17, 2019.

10. Pierre Gurdjian, "Why Leadership Development Programs Fail," *McKinsey & Company Quarterly* (January 2014), https://www.mckinsey.com /featured-insights/leadership/why-leadership-development-programs-fail.

11. Lafley, telephone interview.

12. Jeffrey Dyer, Hal Gregersen, and Clay Christensen, "The Innovator's DNA," *Harvard Business Review*, December 2009,; Clay Christensen, Jeffrey Dyer, and Hal Gregersen, *The Innovator's DNA: Mastering the Five Skills of Disruptive Innovators* (Boston: Harvard Business School Publishing, 2011).

13. Gary Wolf, "Steve Jobs: The Next Insanely Great Thing," *Wired*, February 1, 1996, https://www.wired.com/1996/02/jobs-2/.

14. Graham Winfrey, "Intuit's Scott Cook on the Surprising Source of Massive Growth," *Inc.*, July 25, 2014, https://www.inc.com/graham-winfrey /intuit-s-scott-cook-on-savoring-surprises.html.

15. Christensen, Dyer, and Gregersen, *The Innovator's DNA*.

16. Satya Nadella, *Hit Refresh: The Quest to Rediscover Microsoft's Soul and Imagine a Better Future for Everyone* (New York: HarperBusiness, 2016), 92.

17. David A. Garvin, *Learning in Action: A Guide to Putting the Learning Organization to Work* (Boston: Harvard Business School Press, 2000).

18. Garvin, *Learning in Action*, 39.

19. Satya Nadella, interview by Simon London, "Microsoft's Next Act," *McKinsey Quarterly*, April 2018, https://www.mckinsey.com/industries /technology-media-and-telecommunications/our-insights/microsofts-next -act#.

20. Gustavo Manso, "Motivating Innovation," *Journal of Finance* 66, no. 5 (October 2011): 1823–1860.

21. Peter M. Senge, *The Fifth Discipline: The Art & Practice of the Learning Organization* (New York: Doubleday Business, 1990).

22. Chris Argyris, "Teaching Smart People How to Learn," *Harvard Business Review*, May–June 1991.

23. Carol Dweck, "What Having a 'Growth Mindset' Actually Means" (blog), *Harvard Business Review*, January 13, 2016, https://hbr.org/2016/01 /what-having-a-growth-mindset-actually-means.

24. Ferdz dela Cruz, telephone interview with the authors, June 7, 2018.

25. Nadella, *Hit Refresh*, 100.

26. Andy Hill, interview with the authors, Hollywood, FL, June 26, 2018.

27. Peterson, telephone interview.

28. Chris Groscurth, "Why Your Company Must Be Mission-Driven," *Gallup Workplace*, March 6, 2014, https://www.gallup.com/workplace /236537/why-company-mission-driven.aspx.

29. Scott Anthony, Alasdair Trotter, and Evan Schwartz, "The Top 20 Business Transformations of the Last Decade," *Harvard Business Review*, September 2019.

30. Anthony, Trotter, and Schwartz, "Top 20 Business Transformations."

31. Senge, *Fifth Discipline*, 192.

Chapter 8

1. Thomas Jefferson, "Letter to John Holmes, April 22, 1820," Library of Congress (website), accessed October 20, 2019, https://www.loc.gov /exhibits/jefferson/159.html.

2. Bradley Sawyer and Daniel McDermott, "How Does the Quality of the U.S. Healthcare System Compare to Other Countries?," Peterson-Kaiser Healthcare System Tracker, March 28, 2019, https://www .healthsystemtracker.org/chart-collection/quality-u-s-healthcare-system -compare-countries/#item-start.

3. Christopher Klein, "The Epic Road Trip That Inspired the Interstate Highway System," History.com, June 29, 2016, https://www.history.com /news/the-epic-road-trip-that-inspired-the-interstate-highway-system.

4. Eric Schmitt, "Iraq-Bound Troops Confront Rumsfeld over Lack of Armor," *New York Times*, December 8, 2004, https://www.nytimes.com /2004/12/08/international/middleeast/iraqbound-troops-confront -rumsfeld-over-lack-of.html.

5. "'Stand-To!' The Official Focus of the US Army," Army Futures Command, March 28, 2018, https://www.army.mil/standto/2018-03-28.

6. Abigail Hess, "Harvard Business School Professor: Half of American Colleges Will be Bankrupt in 10 to 15 Years," CNBC, August 30, 2011, https:// www.cnbc.com/2018/08/30/hbs-prof-says-half-of-us-colleges-will-be -bankrupt-in-10-to-15-years.html.

7. Peter Drucker, *Managing in Turbulent Times* (New York: Harper & Row, 1980), 45.

8. Rodd Wagner, "New Evidence That the Peter Principle Is Real—and What to Do about It," *Forbes*, April 10, 2018, https://www.forbes.com/sites /roddwagner/2018/04/10/new-evidence-the-peter-principle-is-real-and -what-to-do-about-it/#54e482691809.

9. "Our Credo," Johnson & Johnson website, https://www.jnj.com /credo/.

10. "Tylenol and the Legacy of J&J's James Burke," *Knowledge at Wharton*, October 2, 2012, https://knowledge.wharton.upenn.edu/article /tylenol-and-the-legacy-of-jjs-james-burke/.

11. John Maynard Keynes, *A Tract on Monetary Reform* (London: Macmillan & Co., 1923), 80.

Epilogue

1. Jeffrey Bezos, "1997 Shareholder Letter," Amazon, accessed October 21, 2019, https://ir.aboutamazon.com/static-files/589ab7fe-9362 -4823-a8e5-901f6d3a0f00.

2. Steven Levy, "Jeff Bezos Owns the Web in More Ways Than You Think," *Wired*, November 13, 2011, https://www.wired.com/2011/11/ff _bezos/.

3. Netflix, S-1, filed with SEC, March 6, 2002, https://www.nasdaq .com/markets/ipos/filing.ashx?filingid=1785401.

4. Google, S-1, filed with SEC, April 29, 2004, https://www.sec.gov /Archives/edgar/data/1288776/000119312504073639/ds1.htm.

5. Bob Johansen, from transcript of Innosight's CEO Summit, Lexington, MA, August 2018.

6. Derek Thompson, "The History of Sears Predicts Nearly Everything Amazon Is Doing," *The Atlantic*, September 25, 2017, https://www .theatlantic.com/business/archive/2017/09/sears-predicts-amazon /540888/.

7. Eugene Kim, "Jeff Bezos to Employees: 'One Day, Amazon Will Fail,' but Our Job Is to Delay It as Long as Possible," CNBC, November 15, 2018, https://www.cnbc.com/2018/11/15/bezos-tells-employees-one-day -amazon-will-fail-and-to-stay-hungry.html.

8. Scott D. Anthony, S. Patrick Viguerie, Evan Schwartz, and John Van Landeghem, "2018 Corporate Longevity Forecast: Creative Destruction Is Accelerating," *Innosight Executive Briefing*, accessed October 21, 2019, https://www.innosight.com/wp-content/uploads/2017/11/Innosight -Corporate-Longevity-2018.pdf.

9. Jeffrey Bezos, "Amazon, 2017 Annual Letter to Shareholders," SEC (website), accessed October 21, 2019, https://www.sec.gov/Archives/edgar /data/1018724/000119312517120198/d373368dex991.htm.

10. Charles Handy, *The Age of Unreason* (Boston: Harvard Business School Press, 1989), 226–227.

11. Seth Klarman, "Hard Choices," Harvard Business School Alumni (website), December 1, 2018, https://www.alumni.hbs.edu/stories/Pages /story-bulletin.aspx?num=6818.

12. Bekele Geleta, "What Is Stewardship, and Should All Great Leaders Practice It?," *New York Times in Education*, accessed October 21, 2019, https://nytimesineducation.com/spotlight/what-is-stewardship-and -should-all-great-leaders-practice-it/.

Index

The letters *t* and *f* following page numbers denote tables and figures, respectively.

Acknowledgments

This book's long journey from rough ideas to printed words on a page began in the late 1990s, when Mark, then a consultant at Booz Allen Hamilton, began working with Harvard Business School's Professor David Garvin on what they called "learning-based strategic planning." This formed the foundation of what was further developed at Innosight to become the future-back way of thinking and planning that we explain in these pages.

Many of our Innosight colleagues contributed to the concept and practice of future-back, too many to name all of them here. Together, across many dozens of client engagements, we have shaped future-back thinking into a powerful and repeatable methodology, and everyone at Innosight deserves some share of the credit.

We want to particularly acknowledge David Duncan, Erika Meldrim, and Prashant Srivastava, who helped shape the future-back methodology in its early days. Scott Anthony, Patrick Viguerie, and Bernard Kümmerli provided very careful reviews of the book in its various stages; and Natalie Painchaud, Tim Riser, Annie Garofalo, Jason Lee, Emily Ottman, Cathy Olofson, and Kristen Blake offered invaluable contributions and critiques.

We also want to thank the many business leaders and executives who have entrusted us with the privilege of helping them bring their visionary strategies to life. Learning runs both ways in these engagements. Challenging, collaborating with, and inspiring us every day, they have all made immeasurable contributions to our thinking.

Roy Davis, a former Johnson & Johnson senior executive and a current member of Innosight's board of advisors, has been a great friend and an invaluable partner in our work on vision and strategy over the years and also in the work of developing the future-back methodology; in fact, he introduced the phrase "future-back" to our lexicon. Innosight Board Advisor Clark Gilbert's careful readings of the book's upfront chapters were extremely helpful.

Bill Hait, Ben Wiegand, Avi Spira, Dave Yazujian, Cat Oyler, Oliver Stohlmann, and their talented teams at Johnson & Johnson continue to inspire us with their quest to intercept disease. They are true future-back visionaries, and we are grateful to have had the opportunity to work with them on their ambitious mission and to tell part of their still-unfolding story.

Chris Chadwick, John Casesa, Lloyd Baird, Karl Ronn, Peter Koen, Michael Putz, Mary Ann Knaus, Mark Harris, Janice Evans, Carolynn Cameron, Scott Cook, Sandi Peterson, Leslie Jelalian, Tony Tiernan, John Grace, Jack London, and Andy Hill are among the many business leaders, teachers, and thinkers who contributed insights at different stages of the book. In particular, former Procter & Gamble chairman and CEO A. G. Lafley read the manuscript and shared his in-depth, invaluable perspectives on it.

Huron Consulting's CEO Jim Roth, President Mark Hussey, Managing Director in Higher Education Practice Peter Stokes, and Managing Director in Huron's Studer Group Leadership Practice Craig Deao, all provided very helpful guidance as well.

On the publishing end, Mark's agent James Levine, publicists Mark Fortier and Jill Totenberg, and freelance editors Andrea Ovans, Heather Hunt, and Bronwyn Fryer contributed excellent advice that helped to focus the manuscript. Our primary editor at Harvard Business Review Press, Kevin Evers, really got us on our way, having enough faith in us to sign us up as authors and providing us with thoughtful, caring guidance throughout the entire book-writing process. We're also grateful to HBR's Allison Peter for her invariably wise assistance. Ash Devillan and Micah Burger at OPX Design and Crystal Spanakos of Innosight created eye-catching graphics and also helped with the overall design of the book.

Arthur Goldwag helped enormously in the sometimes mystical task of taking ideas out of Mark's head and putting them on paper. Their collaboration began well before the book was envisioned, never mind formally proposed, and continued through its many pivots and drafts. He was patient throughout and ever-vigilant that we told the story right.

We also owe a very special thanks to Jake Gulisane, who shepherded so many important elements of the manuscript through its development. And Carly White, Mark's executive assistant, has been an incredible partner in helping manage all the moving pieces of bringing a book together.

Josh would like to thank Mark for his many years of mentorship and for his invitation to join this project; his Innosight colleagues, who never cease to inspire him; and most importantly, his family. He dedicates his portion of this book to them: his parents, Bernie and Simone Suskewicz, for instilling a love of learning and an abiding sense of purpose; his children Rose and Salem, for bringing light into his life every day; and his wife Rachel, his partner in everything and the love of his life.

And finally, Mark's deepest gratitude goes to his wife, Jane Clayson Johnson, his most trusted truth-teller and dearest friend, who has been a tremendous source of wisdom and support throughout the long process of researching, writing, and rewriting *Lead from the Future*. Not only has she patiently endured his many years of distraction, but she has never ceased to remind him of the need to stay focused on his (and what should be everyone's) ultimate goal—to secure a better world for their children, their grandchildren, and their children after them.

About the Authors

Mark W. Johnson cofounded the strategy and innovation management consultancy Innosight with Harvard Business School professor Clayton M. Christensen in 2000 (which was acquired by the Huron Consulting Group in 2017). The author of *Reinvent Your Business Model: How to Seize the White Space for Transformative Growth* (2018) and a coauthor of *Dual Transformation: How to Reposition Today's Business While Creating the Future* (2017), Mark has written and cowritten numerous articles for a wide range of publications, including the McKinsey Award–winning "Reinventing Your Business Model" for *Harvard Business Review.* Prior to Innosight, Mark was a nuclear power–trained surface-warfare officer in the US Navy. He received his MBA from Harvard Business School, a master's degree in civil engineering and engineering mechanics from Columbia University, and a bachelor's degree with distinction in aerospace engineering from the US Naval Academy. Mark and his wife Jane Clayson Johnson are the parents of five children and the grandparents of three.

Josh Suskewicz is a partner at Innosight, where he leads its Life Sciences and Medtech practice, working closely with leadership teams on the challenge of nurturing new growth platforms within established organizations. An accomplished teacher and lecturer, he has written on strategy and innovation for *Harvard Business Review, Forbes*, and hbr.org, and contributed to the business textbook *From Strategy to Execution: Turning Accelerated Global Change into Opportunity.* Josh holds an honors degree in English literature from Harvard College and lives with his wife, Rachel; daughter, Rose; and son, Salem in Brooklyn, New York.